**Hamlyn**
London · New York · Sydney · Toronto

# HISTORY OF THE WORLD CUP

Michael Archer

# CONTENTS

The photographs on the end-papers and title page are as follows:

front endpaper **Johan Neeskens** scores the opening goal in the 1974 World Cup Final for Holland by beating West Germany's goalkeeper, Sepp Maier, from the penalty spot.

back endpaper **West Germany's** equalizer in the 1974 World Cup Final, also scored from the penalty spot. Paul Breitner beats Holland's goalkeeper, Jan Jongbloed.

title page **A scene from the opening ceremony of the 1970 World Cup finals in Mexico. Flags and balloons in the Aztec Stadium.**

**Origins and Development** 8
**1930: Uruguay** 9
**1934: Italy** 12
**1938: France** 17
**1950: Brazil** 22
**1954: Switzerland** 26
**1958: Sweden** 33
**1962: Chile** 41
**1966: England** 47
**1970: Mexico** 62
**1974: West Germany** 74

Published by
The Hamlyn Publishing Group Limited
London · New York · Sydney · Toronto
Astronaut House, Feltham,
Middlesex, England

Copyright © The Hamlyn Publishing Group Limited 1978
ISBN 0 600 39400 X

All rights reserved. No part of this publication may be reproduced, stored in a retrieval system, or translated, in any form or by any means, electrical, mechanical, photocopying, recording or otherwise, without the permission of the Hamlyn Publishing Group Limited.

Filmset in England by Tradespools Limited, Frome, England
Printed in England by
Hazell, Watson & Viney Ltd.
Aylesbury, Bucks.

# FOREWORD

*My* World Cup history takes in both ends of the spectrum as far as England is concerned. Everyone of course remembers that brilliant afternoon at Wembley in July 1966 when we beat our old rivals West Germany to win the trophy. It is easier to forget, however, the moment that will live with me just as long – at Belo Horizonte in 1950, in the first World Cup finals after the war, when an England team including Bert Williams, Billy Wright, Jimmy Dickinson, Tom Finney, Stan Mortensen, Wilf Mannion – and Alf Ramsey – lost 1-0 to the part-timers of the United States. I suppose, apart from the incredible performance of the North Koreans in 1966, this remains the biggest upset in the World Cup's colourful history.

That, of course, is the fascination of the World Cup, just as it is the fascination of our own league and cup competitions. There is never a guarantee, however good a side may be, that it will win a particular match. There is always the speculation before a World Cup final series about the players a particular side may have that are truly World class. When at last the countries meet in the finals the secrets become an open book.

Yet, so often, the truly great teams have not won the World Cup. For example, the Brazilians in 1950; those brilliant Hungarians (one of the finest international teams we have ever seen) in 1954; and, in 1974, the Dutch were the outstanding team in the competition.

And just to anticipate your question – yes, we *were* the best team in 1966. We had more World class players than other sides. We had a system of play that made the players into a better team than they might otherwise have been. And they had that most elusive quality, understanding. It's a blend that every manager seeks. If he finds it, he's a happy man.

The World Cup gave me that happiness. It also gave me moments of sadness. I am happy to have shared both. And, when you recall, as you read this book, the bitterness as well as the joy in nearly fifty years of football history, you will realise how our great game brings together widely differing people from right across the globe. And, win, lose or draw, that is vital. It is a lifeline that is offered to the world. May they always take it.

Sir Alf Ramsey

# ORIGINS AND DEVELOPMENT

Soccer's supreme tournament is living proof of the adage that 'from tiny acorns mighty oak trees grow'. Just as the game itself has spread its gospel into virtually every corner of the globe, so correspondingly has the prestige attached to winning the world championship grown out of all recognition.

In its forty-eight-year history, the World Cup entry list has grown from thirteen in 1930 to 106 for the 1978 tournament, and the advent of television, with its satellites spanning the globe, means that the 'live' audience of 90,000 which saw the first final has now grown to one of around 500 million.

The concept of a World Cup soccer tournament was born at the Antwerp Conference in 1920 of the game's governing body, FIFA (The International Federation of Football Associations). And it mostly owed its birth to the man who was elected President of FIFA that year and whose crusading of the idea was recognised in 1946 by naming that first World Cup trophy after him – the French FA President, Jules Rimet.

FIFA was founded in 1904 by six original member countries – Belgium, Denmark, France, Germany, the Netherlands and Switzerland. By 1930 – and the the staging of the first World Cup tournament – that membership had grown to twenty-six but, sadly, politics blighted the inaugural championship. Withdrawals and defections from many of the European members, including all four British associations, limited the finalists to thirteen . . . hardly an auspicious number and even insufficient to form four 'pools' of four teams each. However, that problem was overcome and Uruguay had the distinction of staging the first tournament as well as being the first of four host countries to win it – a worthy way not only to write themselves into soccer's history books but also to celebrate their country's centenary.

Over the years, the format of the finals has varied. In 1930 those four pools produced semi-finalists who met on a straight knock-out basis to produce finalists. In the following two tournaments (in 1934 in Italy and 1938 in France) it was a knock-out system all the way through. In 1950, when the tournament was revived after the Second World War, it reverted to the four-pools system but with the four winners then playing off in a final pool . . . a format which could have made for an anti-climax but which, as it turned out, finished with the hosts, Brazil, playing Uruguay in a final, decisive match before a record 199,854 spectators.

In 1958 in Sweden, 1962 in Chile and 1966 in England it was still a four-group system but this time with two teams from each group going through to a quarter-final stage, from which point it was again a 'sudden death' affair.

In 1970 in Mexico, 'goal difference' rather than goal average' was used to seperate teams level on points. And finally, in West Germany in 1974, *two* further qualifying groups replaced the quarter – and semi-finals, leaving the two winners to play off in the Final and the runners-up competing for third and fourth places.

That is the system that applies in Argentina in 1978. But the World Cup story starts in Uruguay in 1930.

Jules Rimet presenting the trophy named after him to the President of the Uruguayan Football Association after Uruguay's win in 1930. Brazil won this cup outright with their third win in 1970, and the new cup is now known as the World Cup, always its colloquial name.

# 1930 URUGUAY

FIFA membership: 41

World Cup entrants: 13

Finals: Four games – winners into semi-finals

Leading scorer: Stabile (Argentina) 8 goals

Winners: Uruguay

---

The poor line-up for these first World Cup finals was in spite of Uruguay's pledge to pay the expenses of all competing nations. One by one the top European nations thought better of the long journey – it took three weeks by sea in those days – until eventually there were only five non-South-American teams in the tournament. The European challenge was reduced to second-rate sides, and a measure of its informality was that the French only decided to come four weeks before their boat sailed. As for Rumania, it was only thanks to King Carol that they were represented. He not only picked the team but personally secured the release of the players from their firms – notably the big English oil company which had threatened any players who went with dismissal. The other challenger to the might of the South Americans was the United States. Although the game had never caught on properly there, it had attracted a useful collection of imported players, like the Scot Alex Jackson, a championship winner with Huddersfield in 1926 and a member of the legendary Scottish 'Wembley Wizards' side of 1928 which beat England 5-1. Nevertheless, it was a very muscular and physical team, which earned itself the nickname of 'the shot-putters' from its French rivals.

Uruguay could hardly have started hotter favourites to win their own tournament. They had won the last two Olympic titles, beating Switzerland in the 1924 Final, and Argentina, after a replay, to retain their title in 1928. They had built a magnificent new stadium in Montevideo (incredibly in the space of eight months) and who was to say that it would not be the stage for yet another triumph.

The way the Uruguayans prepared was as thorough as a later generation of Brazilian footballers went about underlining *their* World supremacy. They spent two months 'in concentration' in a luxury hotel in the middle of the Prado Park in Montevideo. And the almost monastic regime cost their brilliant goalkeeper Mazzali, one of their Olympic stars, *his* place in history when he sneaked back to his room one night after curfew and was promptly sent home.

Nonetheless, even with Ballesteros replacing him, Uruguay were an impressive outfit. Their 'Iron Curtain' half-back line of Jose Andrade, Lorenzo Fernandez and Alvaro Gestido were its backbone. Behind, as captain and right-back, strode Jose Nasazzi, and in attack they could boast two brilliant veterans in Hector Scarone and Pedro Petrone.

All form suggested that neighbours Argentina would be Uruguay's strongest challengers, a fact underlined by the closeness of that 1928 Olympic Final in Amsterdam (1-1 and 2-1). Although Juventus of Italy had since lured away their brilliant left winger Raimondo Orsi, they could still build a formidable side around the ruthless, attacking centre half Luisito Monti ('The Man Who Strolls') of Boca Juniors. He too would later join Juventus and, with Orsi, help *Italy* win the next World Cup!

There was a touch of farce about the start of the Argentina challenge. In their first match, against France, they were clinging onto the slender lead of a goal by Monti – scored from a freekick only three minutes earlier – when the referee blew for time six minutes early. The protesting French pointed out his error and the pitch was duly cleared so that the formality of the remaining time could be completed, although many observers, including the watching Uruguayans, thought France were unlucky to lose. In their next match, Argentina beat Mexico 6-3 in a crazy game distinguished by the over-generous awarding of five penalties by the Bolivian referee, Mr Ulysses Saucedo. And so to Argentina's next match with Chile in which Monti and his rugged side got involved in a brawl just before half-time which had to be quelled by police. Stabile, who finished as top scorer for the tournament, got a second goal for Argentina in the second half and they eventually prevailed 3-1.

Meanwhile, Uruguay hardly made an impressive start against Peru. The Peruvians had given no cause for concern in their first match against King Carol's Rumanians, losing 3-1 in a laxly refereed game in which Rumania's full-back Steiner broke a leg and Peru's captain De Las Casas was sent off.

For the crowd in the Centenary Stadium, which was completed only just before the game, Uruguay v Peru was a frustrating affair. In the end a second-half goal by centre-forward Castro settled it. Both Castro and Petrone were rested for the next game against Rumania and the reshuffle worked to the tune of a 4-0 home win.

In the other groups, the United States and Yugoslavia emerged. The Americans with six ex-British professionals in their side won both their matches (against Belgium and Paraguay) 3-0. The latter gave their semi-final opponents Argentina something to think about, since Paraguay had beaten Uruguay in their last international before the World Cup. The Yugoslav triumph over the fancied Brazilians was a major surprise. Tirnanic and Beck put them two-up in half an hour and the best Brazil could do was pull

right **the captains of Uruguay and Argentina, Jose Nazassi and 'Nolo' Fereyra shake hands before the 1930 Final. The referee, centre, is Jean Langenus and the linesmen Henry Christophe and Ulysses Saucedo.**

below **The winning Uruguayan team: Alvaro Gestido, Jose Nazassi, Enrique Ballestrero, Ernesto Masqueroni, Jose Andrade, Lorenzo Fernandez, Pablo Dorado, Hector Scarone, Hector Casstro, Pedro Cea and Santos Iriarte.**

10

one back through Neto. Beck got two more in the comfortable 4-0 win over the other team in the group, Bolivia. So it was Argentina *v* the United States in one semi-final and Uruguay *v* Yugoslavia in the other.

The Americans, rather surprisingly, started as favourites. But the 'shot-putters', for all their strength, mobility and British skill, could not hold the Argentinians after half-time. Argentina led by a goal from Monti at the break, and three goals in a nine-minute spell broke the States' resistance, Stabile getting two of them, and it finished a 6-1 massacre.

Uruguay also ground down the challenge of the Yugoslavs by the same score, but they had to recover from the shock of falling behind in four minutes to a brilliant goal by Seculic. The Uruguayans replied with goals from Cea and Anselmo—one of them clearly offside—and the Yugoslavs might have got back into the match had they not had an apparently good goal disallowed. By half-time it was 3-1 and in the second half Uruguay came somewhere near their best to add three further goals.

So—another Uruguay *v* Argentina final. Boatloads of Argentinian fans poured across the River Plate the night before to be met by police, who searched them for pistols. The crowd capacity was reduced by 10,000 to 90,000 for safety reasons. But, for all the misgivings, the only controversy surrounded the ball. Both sides wanted to supply their own. However, diplomacy triumphed. The Belgian referee, Jean Langenus, appeared on the pitch with a ball under each arm. They would each be used for one half. The Argentinians won the toss; theirs was used first and it produced them a 2-1 half-time lead.

Uruguay scored first through Dorado. But Peucelle equalised and then Stabile, despite offside appeals by Nasazzi, added a second for Argentina. In the fifty-fifth minute Pedro Cea dribbled through for a brilliant equaliser. Ten minutes later Santos Iriarte put Uruguay in front and finally the restored Castro smashed in a fourth. The Cup went to Uruguay. It had been well won. Yet they would not compete in another World Cup for twenty years—and then they would win it again.

Peucelle's shot beats the Uruguayan goalkeeper to put Argentina level in the Final.

### 1st WORLD CUP Uruguay, 1930

| GROUP 1 | | | |
|---|---|---|---|
| France | (3)4 | Mexico | (0)1 |
| Laurent, Langiller | | Carreno | |
| Maschinot 2 | | | |
| Argentina | (0)1 | France | (0)0 |
| Monti | | | |
| Chile | (1)3 | Mexico | (0)0 |
| Vidal, Subiabre 2 | | | |
| Chile | (0)1 | France | (0)0 |
| Subiabre | | | |
| Argentina | (3)6 | Mexico | (0)3 |
| Stabile 3, Verallo 2, | | Lopez, Rosas (F), | |
| Zumelzu | | Rosas (M) | |
| Argentina | (2)3 | Chile | (1)1 |
| Stabile 2, Evansto (M) | | Subiabre | |

|  | P | W | D | L | F | A | Pts |
|---|---|---|---|---|---|---|---|
| Argentina | 3 | 3 | 0 | 0 | 10 | 4 | 6 |
| Chile | 3 | 2 | 0 | 1 | 5 | 3 | 4 |
| France | 3 | 1 | 0 | 2 | 4 | 3 | 2 |
| Mexico | 3 | 0 | 0 | 3 | 4 | 13 | 0 |

| GROUP 2 | | | |
|---|---|---|---|
| Yugoslavia | (2)2 | Brazil | (0)1 |
| Tirnanic, Beck | | Neto | |
| Yugoslavia | (0)4 | Bolivia | (0)0 |
| Beck 2, Marianovic, | | | |
| Vujadinovic | | | |
| Brazil | (1)4 | Bolivia | (0)0 |
| Visintainer 2, Neto 2 | | | |

|  | P | W | D | L | F | A | Pts |
|---|---|---|---|---|---|---|---|
| Yugoslavia | 2 | 2 | 0 | 0 | 6 | 1 | 4 |
| Brazil | 2 | 1 | 0 | 1 | 5 | 2 | 2 |
| Bolivia | 2 | 0 | 0 | 2 | 0 | 8 | 0 |

| GROUP 3 | | | |
|---|---|---|---|
| Romania | (1)3 | Peru | (0)1 |
| Staucin 2, Barbu | | Souza | |
| Uruguay | (0)1 | Peru | (0)0 |
| Castro | | | |
| Uruguay | (4)4 | Romania | (0)0 |
| Dorado, Scarone, | | | |
| Anselmo, Cea | | | |

|  | P | W | D | L | F | A | Pts |
|---|---|---|---|---|---|---|---|
| Uruguay | 2 | 2 | 0 | 0 | 5 | 0 | 4 |
| Romania | 2 | 1 | 0 | 1 | 3 | 5 | 2 |
| Peru | 2 | 0 | 0 | 2 | 1 | 4 | 0 |

| GROUP 4 | | | |
|---|---|---|---|
| USA | (2)3 | Belgium | (0)0 |
| McGhee 2, Patenaude | | | |
| USA | (2)3 | Paraguay | (0)0 |
| Patenaude 2, Florie | | | |
| Paraguay | (1)1 | Belgium | (0)0 |
| Pena | | | |

|  | P | W | D | L | F | A | Pts |
|---|---|---|---|---|---|---|---|
| USA | 2 | 2 | 0 | 0 | 6 | 0 | 4 |
| Paraguay | 2 | 1 | 0 | 1 | 1 | 3 | 2 |
| Belgium | 2 | 0 | 0 | 2 | 0 | 4 | 0 |

**SEMI-FINALS**

| Argentina | (1)6 | USA | (0)1 |
|---|---|---|---|
| Monti, Scopelli, | | Brown | |
| Stabile 2, Peucelle 2 | | | |

| Uruguay | (3)6 | Yugoslavia | (1)1 |
|---|---|---|---|
| Cea 3, Anselmo 2, | | Seculic | |
| Iriarte | | | |

**FINAL**: Montevideo 30.7.30
Attendance 100,000

| Uruguay | (1)4 | Argentina | (2)2 |
|---|---|---|---|
| Dorado, Cea, Iriarte, | | Peucelle, Stabile | |
| Castro | | | |

**Uruguay**: Ballesteros; Nasazzi (capt), Mascheroni; Andrade, Fernandez, Gestido; Dorado, Scarone, Castro, Cea, Iriarte

**Argentina**: Botasso; Della Torre, Paternoster; Evaristo (J), Monti, Suarez; Peucelle, Varallo, Stabile, Ferreira (capt), Evaristo (M)

**Referee**: Langenus (Belgium)

**LEADING SCORERS**:
8—Stabile (Argentina)
5—Cea (Uruguay)
4—Subiabre (Chile)

# 1934 ITALY

FIFA membership: 46

Entrants: 29

Finals: Knock-out

Grounds: Rome, Florence, Naples, Turin, Trieste.

Leading scorers: Schiavio (Italy), Nejedly (Czechoslovakia), Conen (Germany) 4 goals

Winners: Italy

Home advantage had helped Uruguay to victory in 1930 but few had cause to dispute that they were the best team on that occasion. Italy's win four years later was far more blatantly achieved. The Belgian referee, Jean Langenus, who had refereed the 1930 Final said: 'Italy wanted to win. It was natural but they made it far too obvious.' Not for the first, or last time, sport was a platform to advertise a political regime. Mussolini's Fascist Italy wanted to take on and beat the world. This they did—just.

Their first battle was to win the right to stage the tournament. It took eight FIFA congresses before the Italian promise—to run it at a loss if necessary—got them the vote. The line-up this time was much more impressive. For the first time there had to be a preliminary competition to produce the sixteen finalists—and this time the finals were played on a knock-out basis throughout, a fact which meant that South America's sole representatives, Brazil and Argentina, played one match only.

Yes, Europe was back in the driving seat. Uruguay refused to compete. They had been snubbed by the Europeans four years earlier, so this was their retaliation. But, more significantly, they also had a players' strike on their hands. Argentina sent a mere shadow of the side that fought out the Final in 1930; it was a team of reserves. They were afraid that their top stars would be poached by the Italians—and they had good cause to be wary. They had lost their brilliant winger Orsi before the 1930 finals; now even their winning captain of that year, Luisito Monti, had been lured into the Italian fold. He was now the linchpin of a side managed by one of the game's legendary and ample figures, Vittorio Pozzo. Monti, Orsi and the other winger, Guaita, all qualified for Italy as 'oriundi', the sons of Italians.

But where would the main challenge come from, if clearly not from South America? Well, the Italians 'seeded' eight fancied teams . . . they themselves, the two South American sides, Czechoslovakia, Hungary, Austria, Germany and the Netherlands. Of these, on paper, the biggest threat should have come from Austria, a side managed by another 'father figure', Hugo Meisl. His 'Wunderteam' had come very close to denting England's unbeaten home record in a famous match at Stamford Bridge. But, more significantly as a guideline to form, they had beaten Italy 4-2 in Turin the previous February. But it was said they were now a tired team and that Meisl was convinced they could not win.

Italy would learn in the semi-final that they were a team to be taken seriously. Austria were a skilful, delicate side with brilliant players like Matthias Sindelar, a centre-forward nicknamed 'The Man of Paper' and Smistik, a fine, attacking centre-half to rival Monti. Hungary practised the same close control and skill as the Austrians and also had an outstanding centre-forward in the lawyer, Dr Georges Sarosi. Spain, surprisingly, were not seeded but had a difficult side to beat, captained by their veteran goalkeeper Ricardo Zamora. Funnily enough, the Czechs too had an equally famous goalkeeper-captain in Planicka and, for Italy, goalkeeper Combi shared the captaincy with full-back Rosetta.

With Mussolini watching approvingly, Italy kicked off the competition by demolishing the United States 7-1 to make a Roman holiday. It was all so easy. The Americans were nowhere near the side of 1930 and Schiavio, the Italian centre-forward whose goal would eventually win the Final, began with a hat-trick. The Americans' goal came from Donelli, a Neapolitan who was in fact the only player from the finals who stayed on to play in Italy.

In Florence, there was another hat-trick for the German centre-forward Conen as his team swept aside the Belgians 5-2 after an unconvincing start. Argentina's exit was at the hands of Sweden, 3-2. They were handicapped by poor goalkeeping by Freschi and undoubtedly lost to a better team, but at least scored two fabulous

above **Ricardo Zamora, famous goalkeeper and captain of Spain in 1934.**

right **Two views of the goal which beat Austria's 'Wunderteam' in the 1934 semi-final. Above, Guiata of Italy squeezes the ball past the Austrian goalkeeper, and** below, **finishes in the net as the ball follows him in.**

goals. The first was a thundering 25-yard free kick from left-back Belis, to open the scoring; the second, by Galateo, climaxed a brilliant run. Kroon got Sweden's match-winner after two equalisers from Jonasson.

Brazil lost 3-1 without much of a struggle to Spain in Genoa, with De Brito (later to be the mentor of Pelé) missing a penalty. Spain led 3-1 at half-time and that is the way it finished. The Czechs were not convincing as they disposed of a promising Rumanian side 2-1. They could thank their captain Planicka for restricting Rumania to a 1-0 lead at half-time and goals by Puc and Nejedly saw them through eventually.

In Milan, Switzerland upset the seedings by knocking out the Dutch 3-2 with two goals by Kielholz. And, in Naples, the Hungarians had revenge for an astonishing Olympic defeat ten years earlier by beating Egypt 4-2. For those with a phonetic sense of humour it is difficult to resist the name of the Egyptian goalkeeper that day – Moustafa Kamel!

But the surprise of the first round was the performance of France in pushing Austria all the way before losing 3-2 by what was even conceded, years later by

Schall, the scorer, to have been an offside goal. The French could well have gone into the lead in the first minute but for a brilliant save by Austria's goalkeeper, Peter Platzer. The decisive blow to France, however, was the injury to their captain and centre-forward Jean Nicolas. He switched to the wing, scored almost at once but saw his side succumb to that Schall goal in extra time after dominating the second half of the match.

The next hurdle for Italy was the quarter-final draw in Florence against Spain – Zamora and all. The number of occasions in the past when the great Spanish goalkeeper had frustrated them gave them good cause for concern. And so it turned out. At times he seemed to be playing Italy on his own. His bravery was outstanding and, in the face of some ridiculously weak refereeing, it earned Spain a draw after extra-time but cost him his place in the replay played the very next day.

Spain in fact led at half-time through a mishit shot by Regueiro which deceived Combi. Ferrari sent the game into extra-time but only because Schavio impeded Zamora. As the game went on the physical violence increased, so much so that Spain had to replace seven of their side for the replay and Italy four.

The replay was, if anything, more spinelessly refereed than the first encounter. The Spanish outside left, Bosch, was crippled in just five minutes; Spain's two full-backs managed to knock each other out as they raced to cut out an Italian forward and, to compound Spain's misfortunes, they had two goals disallowed. Hardly surprisingly, with the fates so against them, that they succumbed eventually to a header from a corner by Meazza. There were many who felt that a fully fit Spain could have won the Cup; it was little consolation to them that the Swiss referee, Mercet, was later suspended by his own national association.

Violence also infected the quarter-final between those age-old rivals Austria and Hungary. Hugo Meisl described it as 'a brawl, not a football match'. His trump card on this occasion was the introduction of a dashing new forward, Horwath, who crowned a fine movement by putting Austria in front after only seven minutes. Six minutes after half-time it was 2-0, with the goal coming from Zischek. Sarosi pulled it back to 2-1 from the penalty spot but the handicap of having their right winger Markos sent off was too much for Hungary.

Meanwhile, the Germans marched methodically but uninspiringly into the semi-finals with a 2-1 win over Sweden in heavy rain in Milan, with both the goals coming from inside right Hohmann. But undoubtedly the outstanding quarter-final was between Czechoslovakia and Switzerland in Turin. Again Planicka added to his reputation in the Czech goal as the Swiss played well above theirs. Kielholz gave them a breakaway lead in eighteen minutes but Svoboda equalised before half-time. Sobotka put the Czechs in front only for Abegglen to pull it back to 2-2 for Switzerland. Finally, Nejedly got the goal which earned Czecho-

14

above **The Czechoslovakian goal in the 1934 Final. The Italian captain Combi dives but fails to stop a shot from Puc, who had just returned to the field to take a corner.**

opposite **Before the 1934 Final against Czechoslovakia in Rome the Italian team raise their right arms in the Fascist salute.**

slovakia their semi-final place with seven minutes left.

Milan was again blighted by heavy rain for the Italy v Austria semi-final, heavy conditions all against the close skills of the Austrians. Guaita, Italy's right winger, got the only goal of the game in the first half, Zischek racing through alone in the very last minute only to shoot wide. In fairness to them the Italians showed amazing stamina, considering their hard replay against Spain just two days before, and the Austrians did not so much as muster a shot at goal until the forty-second minute. So, exit the 'Wunderteam'. Italy were through to the Final.

In the other semi-final in Rome, the Czechs were far too quick and subtle for the plodding Germans, who badly missed the injured Hohmann. Czechoslovakia deservedly went ahead in twenty-one minutes through Nejedly, who followed up when Junek's shot was parried. But they had to overcome the trauma of a freak German equaliser in the sixty-third minute, when the great Planicka inexplicably allowed Noack's lob to sail over his head – a precursor of the Final. It was enough to give the Germans heart, but the balance was restored when Puc's mighty free kick rattled against the German bar and Krcil scored from the rebound. And then Nejedly made absolutely sure by dribbling through for the third goal. So – an Italy v Czechoslovakia final, preceded by Germany beating Austria 3-2 in the first of a series of those rarely inspired third/fourth place play-offs. The Germans had the incredible boost of scoring in twenty-four seconds.

What a Final it was. The Czechs blended their skill and consistency as never before in the tournament, with Cambal, their attacking centrehalf, and goalkeeper Planicka back to their best in defence, and Puc and Svoboda menacing in front of goal. But the Italians were playing to prove something as Mussolini looked on. Ferrari and Meazza kept the attack on the move, Orsi and Guaita were lively on the wings

15

and Monti tackled ruthlessly. For seventy minutes it was goalless.

Then Puc, who had limped off earlier with cramp, returned to take a corner. The ball ran to him and a first-time shot hurtled back past Combi. 1-0 to Czechoslovakia. Some Italian fans were driven to such hysteria that they grabbed one of the Czech players' hair through the wire netting before the soldiers set him free.

Eight minutes from time came Italy's extraordinary equaliser. Orsi took a pass from Guaita, feinted to shoot with his left, shot instead with his right, and saw the ball curl and dip diabolically over Planicka and into the net – a fluke goal. Next day Orsi tried to repeat it twenty times with an empty goal and failed every time. So the Italians were reprieved. The game went into extra-time.

Even with Meazza limping, the extra half hour was bound to favour the immensely fit home side. And, ironically, Meazza's injury led indirectly to their winning goal. The Czechs were not marking him tightly when, seven minutes into extra-time, he found some space and served Guaita. The final decisive pass reached Schiavio, who skipped past one defender and rifled the World Cup winning shot past Planicka.

Mussolini's grand design had come to pass as he proudly presented Combi with the trophy. To the world outside it had been a travesty of weak refereeing and home advantage turned to fullest possible advantage. 'A sporting fiasco' said Jean Langenus, and few outside Italy would argue.

Full-time in the 1934 Final. Italy had equalized eight minutes from the end, and now manager Vittorio Pozzo, on the left, and captain Combi, centre, discuss with their players the extra time to come, in which Italy scored the winning goal.

### 2nd WORLD CUP Italy, 1934

**FIRST ROUND**
Italy (3)7 USA (0)1
Schiavio 3, Orsi 2, Donelli
Meazza, Ferrari
Czechoslovakia (0)2 Romania (1)1
Puc, Nejedly Dobai
Germany (1)5 Belgium (2)2
Conen 3, Kobierski 2 Voorhoof 2
Austria (1)(1)3 France (1)(1)2
Sindelar, Schall, Nicolas, Verriest
Bican (pen)
Spain (3)3 Brazil (1)1
Iraragorri (pen), Silva
Langara 2

Switzerland (2)3 Netherlands (1)2
Kielholz 2, Abegglen Smit, Vente
Sweden (1)3 Argentina (1)2
Jonasson 2, Kroon Belis, Galateo
Hungary (2)4 Egypt (1)2
Teleky, Toldi 2, Fawzi 2
Vincze

**SECOND ROUND**
Germany (1)2 Sweden (0)1
Hohmann 2 Dunker
Austria (1)2 Hungary (0)1
Horwath, Zischek Sarosi (pen)
Italy (0)(1)1 Spain (1)(1)1
Ferrari Regueiro

Italy (1)1 Spain (0)0
Meazza
Czechoslovakia (1)3 Switzerland (1)2
Svoboda, Sobotka, Kielholz, Abegglen
Nejedly

**SEMI-FINALS**
Czechoslovakia (1)3 Germany (0)1
Nejedly 2, Krcil Noack
Italy (1)1 Austria (0)0
Guaita

**THIRD PLACE MATCH**: Naples
Germany (3)3 Austria (1)2
Lehner 2, Conen Horwath, Seszta

**FINAL**: Rome 10.6.34 Attendance 55,000
Italy (0)(1)2 Czech. (0)(1)1
Orsi, Schiavio Puc
**Italy**: Combi (capt); Monzeglio, Allemandi; Ferraris, Monti, Bertolini; Guaita, Meazza, Schiavio, Ferrari, Orsi
**Czechoslovakia**: Planicka (capt); Zenisek, Ctyroky, Kostalek, Cambal, Kroil; Junek, Svoboda, Sobotka, Nejedly, Puc
**Referee**: Eklind (Sweden)

**LEADING SCORERS**
4—Conen (Germany), Nejedly (Czechoslovakia), Schiavio (Italy)

# 1938 FRANCE

FIFA membership 51

Entries: 26

Finals: Knock-out

Grounds: Parc des Princes and Stade Colombes, Paris; Toulouse; Rheims; Strasbourg; Le Havre; Antibes; Lille; Bordeaux; Marseilles

Leading scorer: Leonidas (Brazil) 8 goals

Winners: Italy

---

Home advantage was beginning to look decisive after two World Cups, but the 1938 finals in France changed all that as Italy held onto their crown, and in far more convincing style than their home victory four years earlier. Manager Pozzo himself considered his 1938 side superior to the earlier one and from it only the inside forwards Meazza and Ferrari survived. Monti had gone, his place going to another South American, Andreolo from Uruguay. The two full-backs from the Olympic-winning side of 1936, Foni and Rava, had moved up. Olivieri had emerged as a worthy successor to Combi in goal, and at centre-forward, the tall, powerful Silvio Piola was launched on an international career which would make him the most prolific Italian scorer of all time. He would pass Meazza's total in 1951, a year before he eventually retired.

The shadow of war hung over Europe and several countries who might have threatened Italy's supremacy were missing from the finals. The four British associations were still split from FIFA; the Nazi occupation of Austria ended that country's chance of competing and enabled the Germans to recruit some of their players; Spain was pre-occupied with a Civil War; Argentina surprisingly withdrew and Uruguay again did not want to know.

For the first time the host and the cup-holder teams both had automatic byes to the final rounds. Again it was a knock-out system and again there were seedings. The 'unknown' outsiders, both making their one and only appearances in the finals, were Cuba and the Dutch East Indies.

Brazil were the sole South American representatives – a much improved side with Leonidas, 'The Black Diamond', the new goal scoring sensation at centre forward. The Czechs still had goalkeeper Planicka, half-back Kostalek and forwards Nejedly and Puc from their 1934 Final side; they had proved their strength a year before in a narrow 5-4 defeat against England in London. Still in a useful-looking Hungarian side was Dr Georges Sarosi, now his country's highest-paid player; he had been switched back to centre forward, playing alongside the promising young Szengeller. And, in a tournament distinguished by great centre forwards, Norway could boast a veritable Viking in the blond Brunylden. France, as hosts, had a useful rather than a brilliant team and, like Germany, had recently gone down at home to England. The Swiss, on the other hand, with Trello Abegglen surviving from their 1934 side, had beaten the touring English 2-1, giving notice that they were to spring some surprises.

Of the seven first-round matches only two failed to go into extra-time and, undoubtedly, the hardest fought tie was between Germany and Switzerland in Paris. Sepp Herberger had taken over a German side demoralised by England's famous 6-3 win in Berlin, and into the team for their first match he drafted four Austrians, one of whom, the outside left Pesser, was sent off. It was a very physical game, and went into extra-time thanks to a headed equaliser from Abegglen, who had hobbled back into the fray after injury just in time to see Gauchel score for Germany from Pesser's cross. Pesser got his marching orders for kicking Minelli on the knee but, otherwise, extra-time produced nothing noteworthy and no goals.

The replay five days later was a real see-saw affair. The Germans included three Austrians this time and recalled their skilful captain of 1934, Szepan, at inside left. They were leading 2-0 by half-time thanks to Hahnemann and an own goal by Loertscher.

A goal by Wallaschek put the Swiss back in it early in the second half but when they lost left wing Abei, their chance seemed to have gone. But soon after Abei returned, Bickel equalised and then Abegglen underlined his brilliance with two fine match-winning goals. 4-2 to Switzerland and Germany were out.

An even greater upset was the defeat of Rumania in Toulouse by the unknown Cubans. Half the Rumanian side had World Cup experience, three from 1930 in Uruguay. They had the experience and tactical skill, the Cubans the speed and control – and in Carvajeles a superb goalkeeper who had conceded only nine goals in the Cuban championship. Cuba actually led 3-2 in extra-time but Dobai earned Rumania their replay.

Astonishingly, Cuba dropped the brilliant Carvajeles, insisting that his replacement Ayra was even better. And so it turned out. They recovered from being a goal down to win 2-1. The winner, according to the French linesman, was offside but the German referee allowed it. But considering they had only qualified because of Mexico's withdrawal, who was to deny Cuba her one moment of World Cup glory? The true facts of life would be learned in the next round!

17

In Le Havre, the Dutch took the Czechs into extra-time but then the loss of inside right Van der Veen in the second half and the absence of their leading scorer Bakhuijs proved too much. Czechoslovakia scored 3-2, two goals from their half-backs and one from the celebrated Nejedly. Italy, the holders, meanwhile had an unexpectedly rough passage against Norway in Marseilles. Ferrari gave Italy a second-minute lead but the Norwegians kept a tight grip on Piola and left their own marauding centre-forward Brunylden to give Andreolo a really torrid time. Three times the Italian woodwork was hit and Olivieri needed to be in brilliant form in the Italian goal. Eventually, Brustad got the Norwegian equaliser but was denied a possible winner for offside before extra-time. It was Piola who had the last word, picking up a rebound to put the Italians through.

The sensation of the first round – certainly from a goalscoring point of view – came on a muddy pitch in Strasbourg with the meeting of Brazil and Poland, a team making their first appearance in the World Cup finals. Brazil had Leonidas and the Poles, one of the most talented inside forwards in Europe, Ernest Willimowski.

A first-half hat-trick by the elusive little Leonidas saw Brazil leading 3-1 at half-time. The second half brought the tall, blonde Willimowski into his own. He duly completed *his* hat-trick to take the game into extra-time at 4-4. In extra-time both Leonidas and Willimowski got their fourth goals but another one by Romeu for Brazil proved decisive. Brazil went through and the Poles sportingly sent them a good luck telegram before their next game.

To complete a memorable first round, the hosts France beat their old rivals Belgium fairly uninspiringly 3-1 in Paris and, at Rheims, Hungary put the Dutch East Indies firmly in their place 6-0 with Sarosi and Szengeller both scoring twice. Even more decisive was the dispatching of Cuba by Sweden in the second round. The Swedes had drawn a first-round bye, so poor old Carvajeles, back in the Cuban goal again, felt the full wrath of a fresh, fit side. All the Swedish forward line scored, with winger Gustav Wetterstroem getting four in the 8-0 massacre of Antibes. The Cubans returned home sadly via New York, where they watched Joe Louis knock out Max Schmeling.

Meanwhile, the Frenchmen in a 58,000 crowd in Paris were hoping their side would administer the same treatment to Italy in a fascinating second-round pairing of hosts and holders. The Italians played in Fascist black but, sadly for French hopes, the side that had held the Italians 0-0 in Paris the previous December played without any colour themselves. They had no answer to the rampant Piola – his two goals in the second half won the game for Italy 3-1 after the French had rashly gambled everything on attack.

In Lille, feeling the strain of the replay with Germany and without key defender Minelli and winger Abei, Switzerland went down 2-0 to the technically superior Hungarians. Szengeller got both the goals to save Hungary's sole selector Dr Diest from having to keep his promise of walking to Budapest if Hungary lost!

The remaining quarter-final

between Czechoslovakia and Brazil, now joint-favourites with Italy; a game which, by an unhappy chance, was chosen to inaugurate the new stadium in Bordeaux, turned out to be one of the great disgraces of World Cup history – bad enough to rank alongside the 1954 'Battle of Berne' when Hungary and Brazil clashed ignominiously. Two Brazilians and a Czech were sent off in Bordeaux; Planicka, the Czech goalkeeper, broke his arm and Nejedly had his leg broken.

Zeze began it all by violently kicking Nejedly early on and rightly getting expelled for it. Nejedly survived to equalise Leonidas' goal on the half hour for Brazil with a second-half penalty. Just before half-time Riha of Czechoslovakia and Machados of Brazil were also sent off for fighting, and it was handball by Da Guia which gave away the penalty with which Nejedly sent the game into extra-time. The depleted Czechs held out against the nine men of Brazil and so the game went to a replay. Mercifully, though, the replay was a far less passionate meeting. The Brazilians had made nine changes; the Czechs six.

Czechoslovakia went ahead through the busy Kopecky but lost him with an injury after twenty-five minutes. The Brazilian fight-back in the second half was decisive. The inevitable Leonidas equalised and Roberto eventually volleyed the winner. But the Czechs could feel hard done by – just before the winning goal, a shot by Senecky certainly appeared to have crossed the line before the Brazilian goalkeeper scooped it away.

In the semi-finals, the Brazilian team manager Pimenta played the astonishing gamble of leaving out both Leonidas and the highly talented Tim from the team to meet Italy in Marseilles. 'We are keeping them for the Final', he boasted, but it was a prophecy that did not come true. Mind you, if defender Domingas da Guia had not fallen prey to a vendetta with Piola, it could have been different. Italy were leading 1-0 from a goal by Colaussi when Domingas da Guia took Piola's legs from under him – penalty! Meazza made no mistake and, although Romeu

opposite **This header from Brazil in the match with Poland looks well covered by the Polish goalkeeper, but the game provided an exciting feast of goals, with Brazil winning 6-5 after extra time.**

above **Brazil played two quarter-final matches with Czechoslovakia – the first a disgraceful draw in which three players were sent off. The scene above shows Brazil attacking the Czech goal in the replay, which they won 2-1 in the new Bordeaux stadium.**

scored in the second half, the Brazilians had met their match, and Leonidas and Tim had been rested in vain.

The other semi-final between Sweden and Hungary was totally one-sided, though few would have guessed it when Sweden, coached by a Hungarian, scored in the first thirty-five seconds through winger Nyberg. Thereafter, though, Sarosi and Szengeller (who scored a hat-trick) carved up the Swedish defence as Hungary hit five goals without further reply. And while they were doing it a bold blackbird obviously decided that the Swedes were unlikely to invade the Hungarian half and spent much of the second half enjoying

corner, before passing to Meazza, who sent Colaussi in for the first goal. In less than a minute Hungary were level with Sarosi finding Titkos in an unmarked position. But it was Hungary's poor marking that proved decisive. Meazza put Piola through to score number two and then laid on a third for Colaussi. Sarosi did manage a token second goal for Hungary in the second half but it was virtually all over now. And, just to make sure, Piola crashed home his second goal and Italy's fourth after a beautiful one-two with Biavati.

Discipline coupled with physical strength and not a little skill had proved a winning formula. It was

opposite, above **Sarosi following up for Hungary as the ball beats the Italian goalkeeper to keep Hungary in the game.**

opposite, below left **Meazza receives the Cup for Italy – their second successive win.**

opposite, below right **Vittorio Pozza holds the Cup as the Italian players celebrate in Paris. From an Italian magazine cover.**

the worms undisturbed!

So it was Italy against Hungary in the Final in the Stade Colombes. Could Sarosi find his peak form and rouse the Hungarians to new heights or would the Italian rhythm and bite be too much for them? The crowds obviously thought the latter since only 45,000 came to the game.

A classic Italian breakaway opened the scoring in six minutes. Biavati ran almost the length of the field, following a Hungarian

a more flexible and attractive blend than in Rome four years earlier, even though team manager Vittorio Pozzo boasted in Paris – 'We played for the Cup, leaving aside all flourishes'.

There would be no World Cup flourishes now until 1950. The world was about to be engulfed by war.

The first three World Cups had firmly established what was to become an international event rivalling the Olympic Games.

above left **Meazza and Sarosi, stalwarts of Italian and Hungarian football, shake hands in front of referee Capdeville before the 1938 Final.**

above **Rava, of Italy, getting in a header during the Final.**

### 3rd WORLD CUP France, 1938

**FIRST ROUND**
Switzerland (1)(1)1 Germany (0)(1)1
Abegglen — Gauchel
Switzerland (0)4 Germany (2)2
Wallaschek, Bickel, — Hahnemann,
Abegglen 2 — Loertscher (og)
Cuba (0)(2)3 Romania (1)(2)3
Tunas, Maquina, — Covaci, Baratki,
Sosa — Dobai
Cuba (2)2 Romania (1)1
Socorro, Maquina — Dobai
Hungary (4)6 Dutch East (0)0
Kohut, Toldi, Sarosi 2, — Indies
Szengeller 2
France (2)3 Belgium (1)1
Veinante, Nicolas 2 — Isemborghs

Czecho- (0)(0)3 Nether- (0)(0)0
slovakia — lands
Kostalek, Boucek,
Nejedly
Brazil (3)(4)6 Poland (1)(4)5
Leonidas 4, Peracio, — Willimowski 4,
Romeu — Piontek
Italy (1)(1)2 Norway (0)(1)1
Ferrari, Piola — Brustad

**SECOND ROUND**
Sweden (4)8 Cuba (0)0
Andersson, Jonasson,
Wetterstroem 4,
Nyberg, Keller
Hungary (1)2 Switzerland (0)0
Szengeller 2

Italy (1)3 France (1)1
Colaussi, Piola 2 — Heisserer
Brazil (1)(1)1 Czech. (0)(1)1
Leonidas — Nejedly (pen)
Brazil (0)2 Czech. (1)1
Leonidas, Roberto — Kopecky

**SEMI-FINALS**
Italy (2)2 Brazil (0)1
Colaussi, Meazza (pen) — Romeu
Hungary (3)5 Sweden (1)1
Szengeller 3, Titkos, — Nyberg
Sarosi

**THIRD PLACE MATCH**: Bordeaux
Brazil (1)4 Sweden (2)2
Romeu, Leonidas 2, — Jonasson, Nyberg
Peracio

**FINAL**: Paris 19.6.38 Attendance 65,000
Italy (3)4 Hungary (1)2
Colaussi 2, Piola 2 — Titkos, Sarosi
Italy: Olivieri; Foni, Rava; Serantoni,
Andreolo, Locatelli; Biavati, Meazza (capt),
Piola, Ferrari, Colaussi
Hungary: Szabo; Polgar, Biro, Szalay,
Szucs, Lazar; Sas, Vincze, Sarosi (capt),
Szengeller, Titkos
Referee: Capdeville (France)

**LEADING SCORERS**
8—Leonidas (Brazil)
7—Szengeller (Hungary)
5—Piola (Italy)

# 1950 BRAZIL

FIFA membership: 68

Entries: 28

Finals: Four qualifying groups, plus final four-team pool,

Grounds: Rio de Janeiro, Belo Horizonte, Porto Alegre, Sao Paulo, Curitiba

Leading scorer: Ademir (Brazil) 7 goals

Winners: Uruguay

---

The re-opening of World Cup hostilities in 1950 was marked by the hosts with the building of a mammoth new stadium, which, at 318 metres high and 945 metres in circumference, is to this day the biggest in the world – a veritable temple to the great god soccer. The massive, three-tier building, standing beside and named after the Maracana river in Rio de Janeiro, holds 200,000 spectators, separated from the pitch by a ditch 3 metres wide and 3 metres deep. The way it catered for the world's press and media men as well as the sports requirements – not only soccer – of the local community made it unique at the time. And with that volume of support behind them who could deny Brazil's chances of winning?

The entry list was disappointing. Late withdrawals plus the strange league system format and inept organisation did not help to re-establish the world's greatest soccer tournament after a break of twelve years. This time the four qualifying groups would provide the teams for a final pool which in turn would be run on a league basis with the winner taking the trophy. The idea of playing a single group at one venue had not yet emerged, so everyone, except the hosts, would be involved in travelling vast distances between matches. This was enough to persuade the French to withdraw.

The Austrians, on the other hand, said their team was 'too young' and then proceeded to beat Italy in Vienna on the eve of the tournament. Germany were still excluded from FIFA so they too were missing, along with Russia, Hungary, Czechoslovakia and Argentina – who all chose not to compete for various reasons.

Back into the fold, though, came the 1930 winners Uruguay, and for the first time England joined in. FIFA had allowed the British associations two places in the finals to be decided on the results of the Home International Championship, but Scotland decided in advance that they would not go unless they won the championship – and they lost 1-0 at Hampden Park. So England alone carried the British flag . . . yet it was to be lowered in the most dramatic and unbelievable way. England and Brazil were the favourites to win the title.

Brazil cloistered their talented squad in a house outside Rio, lavishly financed by manufacturers. Their manager, on a reputed salary of £1,000 a month, was Flavio Costa, the moustachioed boss of the Vasco da Gama club in Rio. With him he had two doctors, two masseurs and three chefs. England, typical of their 'divine right' attitude, did not even bring a doctor. But they brought a lot of talent. It was a side of giants like wingers Stanley Matthews and Tom Finney, goalkeeper Bert Williams, full-back Alf Ramsey, later to write another personal chapter in England's World Cup history, and that quicksilver inside forward Wilf Mannion. Missing though was a brilliant centre-half, Neil Franklin. He had been lured off that summer to Bogota to join the highly paid new professional league of Colombia which FIFA had outlawed. It cost Franklin his World Cup place and did not earn him much money in the long run.

Italy, winners of the past two tournaments, were bravely there to defend their title but their hopes had crashed with the Superga jet which plunged into the hillside overlooking Turin in May 1949 killing seventeen Torino players, most of them internationals. Vittorio Pozzo had gone too – replaced as *commissario tecnico* the same year. It was the end of an era.

Even though the Maracana Stadium was not quite finished for the opening match, honour was satisfied. Five thousand pigeons fluttered skywards, a twenty-one-gun salute was fired and the hosts Brazil disposed of Mexico by four goals to nil, with Ademir scoring two.

Sao Paulo saw the exit of the Italians. Despite their local support they bowed out 3-2 to Sweden, for whom Hans Jeppson, their blonde centre-forward, got two goals, proving too good even for Italy's elegant centre-half Carlo Parola. Sweden only then needed to draw with Paraguay 2-2 in Curitiba to go through.

Meanwhile, England won their first game 2-0 against Chile with goals from Mortensen and Mannion in Rio. It was said that the muggy air of the Brazilian capital did not suit them, but they would soon have a chance to sample the mountain air of Belo Horizonte. It was not the air but the totally underrated United States team that was to prove the problem.

The Americans had given Spain a good run for their money, leading at half-time before finally losing 3-1 in Curitiba. The States were skippered by Eddie McIlvenny, a Scot who had been given a free transfer by Wrexham of the Third Division (North) only eighteen months before. They also boasted a Belgian left-back and a Haitian centre-forward. But this

Italy's centre-half Carlo Parola, right, could not contain Hans Jeppson, of Sweden, whose two goals helped Sweden knock out holders Italy in 1950.

polyglot collection was about to spring one of the biggest surprises in the World Cup history.

No one gave the Americans the slightest chance. Indeed, half their team stayed up into the small hours the night before the game. Yet on the bumpy, bare Belo Horizonte ground, mighty England fell to a goal after thirty-seven minutes scored with a header by the Haitian Gaetjens from a cross by Bahr. Hard as England pressed they could not break through. It is argued that Jimmy Mullen's header from Alf Ramsey's free kick did cross the line before Borghi scooped it out, but it was not allowed and all England's chances came to nothing. The British public could not believe the scoreline: United States 1 England 0. Now England had to beat Spain in their last game in Rio to survive.

Meanwhile, even Brazil had faltered after their opening victory. Also on the little Belo Horizonte ground, Yugoslavia had already put Switzerland firmly in her place with a 3-0 win, so it was quite a shock to find Brazil struggling to earn a 2-2 draw with the Swiss in Sao Paulo. Indeed, many people thought the Swiss deserved to win. Costa had picked a Brazilian team full of local Sao Paulo players and it very nearly proved a costly gesture. Brazil led 2-1 until two minutes from time when Tamini scored a breakaway goal.

This left Brazil needing to beat Yugoslavia in Rio to qualify for the final pool, since the Yugoslavs had meanwhile disposed of Mexico 4-1 in Porto Alegre. Brazil eventually came through 2-0 but who knows how much closer it might have been if Mitic, the Yugoslav inside right, had not cut his head on a girder as he left the dressing room. He played with it heavily bandaged. In the end, though, it was the Brazilian inside-forward trio of Zizinho, Ademir and Jair, prompted from half-back by Bauer, that won the match. Mitic was still off the field in the third minute when Bauer sent Ademir through to score. And it was Bauer who provided the killer pass for Zizinho to make absolutely sure in the second half.

So Brazil qualified. So too did Uruguay, whose only qualifying game was against Bolivia in Recife, which they won contemptuously 8-0 with Juan Schiaffino scoring four. Sweden's draw with Paraguay had seen them through at the expense of Italy. And that left Spain and England fighting

Sweden's hopes disappeared with a 3-2 defeat by Uruguay, whose goalkeeper is seen catching a high cross.

for the other place. Both sides had beaten Chile 2-0 in Rio, the Chilean attack led throughout by George Robledo, the half-Chilean, half-Yorkshire centre-forward from Newcastle United. Spain had, more realistically, beaten the United States 3-1 in Curitiba, so nothing less than a win would do for England.

They made four changes, bringing in Matthews and two new caps in Eddie Baily and Bill Eckersley. But it was not enough. The other Newcastle striker, Jackie Milburn, had what appeared to be a perfectly good goal disallowed and a second-half goal headed by Zarra sent England crashing out of the tournament.

So Brazil, Spain, Sweden and Uruguay fought out the final pool ... and what a brilliant start the Brazilians made. In their first two matches they put seven past Sweden, with Ademir getting four, and then trounced Spain 6-1. They were irresistible. Their skill and understanding surpassed anything seen in the World Cup before.

George Raynor, the Yorkshire coach who managed Sweden, had planned to surprise Brazil with an early goal. History shows how well that worked! All Sweden got from the massacre was a penalty by Andersson.

Meanwhile, Uruguay were grinding out the main challenge to the hosts. Spain made it difficult for them, though, in a bad-tempered 2-2 draw. Basora managed to escape the attentions of Andrade, nephew of the Andrade in the 1930 winning side, sufficiently to score both Spanish goals. And then Uruguay had to recover from the shock of trailing to Sweden at half-time, also in Sao Paulo. In the end, they outlasted the Swedes. They had had, after all, an infinitely easier passage to the final pool. And on the day, Sweden's Skoglund was off form and winger Johnsson never really recovered from a bad foul by Gonzales. Uruguay scraped through 3-2. Their final match with Brazil would decide the championship.

In effect it was a Final, although Brazil only needed to draw to take the trophy. With two such recent results behind them, not to mention a passionate 200,000 crowd in the Maracana, Brazil had to be favourites. The stage was surely set for yet another home win. Yet Flavio Costa was not overconfident. He knew Uruguay were Brazil's bogey team – and how!

Brazil scintillated with all their earlier brilliance in the first half. Skipper and centre-half Varela marshalled Uruguay's defenders superbly and behind them in inspirational form was goalkeeper Maspoli. He was not beaten until two minutes after half-time when Friaca, the Brazilian winger, finally scored. But Varela pressed forward for the equaliser and after sixty-five minutes it came. Varela started the move, sending Ghiggia hurtling down the right flank. His centre reached the unmarked Schiaffino, who had time to measure his shot – and score.

The Brazilian defence, which up till now had not been really extended, was shown wanting – particularly on the left side. And, sure enough, eleven minutes from time, Ghiggia himself took a return pass from Perez and, cutting in from the wing, squeezed his shot between Barbosa and the near post. Brazil were beaten; a nation mourned. Uruguay were champions again.

above **In the match which decided the winners of the World Cup, Friaca gives Brazil the lead early in the second half.**

left **The winning goal for Uruguay. Ghiggia raises his hands in triumph as his shot beats Barbosa's near post dive.**

### 4th WORLD CUP Brazil, 1950

**GROUP 1**
Brazil (1)4 Mexico (0)0
Ademir 2, Jair
Baltazar
Yugoslavia (3)3 Switzerland (0)0
Tomasevic 2, Oganov
Yugoslavia (2)4 Mexico (0)1
Bobek, Cajkowski 2, Casarin
Tomasevic
Brazil (2)2 Switzerland (1)2
Alfredo, Baltazar Fatton, Tamini
Brazil (1)2 Yugoslavia (0)0
Ademir, Zizinho
Switzerland (2)2 Mexico (0)1
Bader, Fatton Velasquez

| | P | W | D | L | F | A | Pts |
|---|---|---|---|---|---|---|---|
| Brazil | 3 | 2 | 1 | 0 | 8 | 2 | 5 |
| Yugoslavia | 3 | 2 | 0 | 1 | 7 | 3 | 4 |
| Switzerland | 3 | 1 | 1 | 1 | 4 | 6 | 3 |
| Mexico | 3 | 0 | 0 | 3 | 2 | 10 | 0 |

**GROUP 2**
Spain (0)3 USA (1)1
Basora 2, Zarra Souza (J)
England (1)2 Chile (0)0
Mortensen, Mannion
USA (1)1 England (0)0
Gaetjens
Spain (2)2 Chile (0)0
Basora, Zarra
Spain (0)1 England (0)0
Zarra
Chile (2)5 USA (0)2
Robledo, Cremaschi 3, Pariani, Souza (J)
Prieto

| | P | W | D | L | F | A | Pts |
|---|---|---|---|---|---|---|---|
| Spain | 3 | 3 | 0 | 0 | 6 | 1 | 6 |
| England | 3 | 1 | 0 | 2 | 2 | 2 | 2 |
| Chile | 3 | 1 | 0 | 2 | 5 | 6 | 2 |
| USA | 3 | 1 | 0 | 2 | 4 | 8 | 2 |

**GROUP 3**
Sweden (2)3 Italy (1)2
Jeppson 2, Carapellese,
Andersson Muccinelli
Sweden (2)2 Paraguay (1)2
Sundqvist, Palmer Lopez (A), Lopez (F)
Italy (1)2 Paraguay (0)0
Carapellese, Pandolfini

| | P | W | D | L | F | A | Pts |
|---|---|---|---|---|---|---|---|
| Sweden | 2 | 1 | 1 | 0 | 5 | 4 | 3 |
| Italy | 2 | 1 | 0 | 1 | 4 | 3 | 2 |
| Paraguay | 2 | 0 | 1 | 1 | 2 | 4 | 1 |

**GROUP 4**
Uruguay (4)8 Bolivia (0)0
Schiaffino 4, Miguez 2,
Vidal, Ghiggia

| | P | W | D | L | F | A | Pts |
|---|---|---|---|---|---|---|---|
| Uruguay | 1 | 1 | 0 | 0 | 8 | 0 | 2 |
| Bolivia | 1 | 0 | 0 | 1 | 0 | 8 | 0 |

**FINAL POOL**
Uruguay (1)2 Spain (2)2
Ghiggia, Varela Basora 2
Brazil (3)7 Sweden (0)1
Ademir 4, Chico 2, Andersson (pen)
Maneca
Uruguay (1)3 Sweden (2)2
Ghiggia, Miguez 2 Palmer, Sundqvist
Brazil (3)6 Spain (0)1
Jair 2, Chico 2, Igoa
Zizinho, Parra (og)

Sweden (2)3 Spain (0)1
Johnsson, Mellberg Zarra
Palmer
*Uruguay (0)2 Brazil (0)1
Schiaffino, Ghiggia Friaca

| | P | W | D | L | F | A | Pts |
|---|---|---|---|---|---|---|---|
| Uruguay | 3 | 2 | 1 | 0 | 7 | 5 | 5 |
| Brazil | 3 | 2 | 0 | 1 | 14 | 4 | 4 |
| Sweden | 3 | 1 | 0 | 2 | 6 | 11 | 2 |
| Spain | 3 | 0 | 1 | 2 | 4 | 11 | 1 |

**Uruguay**: Maspoli; Gonzales (M), Tejera; Gambetta, Varela (capt), Andrade; Ghiggia, Perez, Miguez, Schiaffino, Moran

**Brazil**: Barbosa; Augusto (capt), Juvenal; Bauer, Danilo, Bigode; Friaca, Zizinho, Ademir, Jair, Chico

**LEADING SCORERS**
7—Ademir (Brazil)
5—Basora (Spain), Schiaffino (Uruguay)

*Deciding match of final pool. Played at Maracana Stadium, Rio de Janeiro, 16.7.50
Attendance: 199,854
**Referee**: Reader (England)

# 1954 SWITZERLAND

FIFA membership: 80

Entries: 36

Finals: Four qualifying groups, quarter-final onwards knock-out

Grounds: Lausanne, Geneva, Zurich, Berne, Basle, Lugano

Leading scorer: Kocsis (Hungary) 11 goals

Winners: West Germany

---

By the time little Switzerland played hosts to the 1954 World Cup, West Germany were back in the international fold and a new soccer power had emerged in Europe. As Holland were to prove twenty years later, a uniquely talented generation can spring up in one country and produce a blend of rare genius in the same side. So it was with Hungary.

England, still licking the wounds of Belo Horizonte, had clung on, with typical 'head in sand' pride, to the self-deception that the country which gave the world the game should be able to play it best. Helping to substantiate the belief was an unbeaten home record. But on a grey November day in 1953, the Hungarians came to Wembley and shattered all the illusions. England and all her outmoded traditions were put to the sword by the most brilliant side Wembley had ever seen. The 6-3 victory scarcely flattered Hungary and when they repeated the slaughter 7-1 in Budapest the following May the message was clear: here was a team ready to take over from the South Americans. It was fit to rule the world – and so it should have done in the 1954 finals but for that wily manager of the West Germans, Sepp Herberger. It is sad in a way that talent alone is often not enough to win; sad too that this World Cup produced a blot on the international scene which has never been forgotten. The 'Battle of Berne', as it came to be called, will be remembered as long as the dramatic Final, played on the same ground.

Hungary came to Switzerland looking full of goals. They had a brilliant attack. At the heart of everything was their little general Ferenc Puskas, a captain with a matchless left foot. Josef Boszik, a member of the Hungarian parliament, attacked from wing-half, Zoltan Czibor was a 'flyer' on the left wing, and there to finish it off were Nandor Hidegkuti, a deep-lying centre-forward, Sandor Kocsis, so superb in the air, or, indeed, Puskas. 'With a left foot like that, who needs a right!' joked England captain Billy Wright after chasing his shadow all over Wembley the previous year.

By comparison the other countries were outsiders in 1954. Austria still had the remnants of a fine team, motivated by Ernst Ocwirk, an imperious, attacking wing-half. Sweden had been robbed of many stars by Italian clubs and was knocked out by Belgium. The Italians themselves had built a formidable defensive system around the Inter Milan 'bloc'. Brazil had lost their incomparable inside-forward trio from 1950. They came, under new manager Zeze Moreira, with two fine full-backs in Djalma Santos and Nilton Santos, and Julinho and Didi as an inspirational right-wing partnership. Yugoslavia would be useful outsiders, too, with the agile Vladimir Beara in goal, Cjaicowski and Boskov (later national team manager) at wing-half and a forward line still boasting Mitic and Bobek from four years before, plus Zebec and

26

Vukas as goalscorers and a brilliant young right winger in Milutinovic. As for England, morale could scarcely be repaired in time, not to mention the gulf in technique that was all too obvious. This, of course, is not to undervalue the skills of wingers Matthews and Finney who were still there and the big, burly centre-forward Nat Lofthouse.

The pool system was a strange one. Of the four teams in each group, two were seeded not to meet each other, i.e. the two 'weak' sides played the two 'strong' ones. Two went through from each group and from the quarter-final stage it became a straight knock-out.

And by another strange quirk of organisation, any game that was drawn at full-time would go into extra-time.

Yugoslavia did not need extra-time in their opening match with France, though only a solitary goal by Milutinovic saw them through. As for the 'minnows' they took a terrible beating. Brazil, orchestrated by the irrepressible Didi, trounced Mexico 5-0, Hungary crushed South Korea 9-0 and West Germany beat Turkey 4-1 without extending themselves.

Both British sides, Scotland playing the World Cup for the first time, missed the chance of a winning start. Scotland, in fact, played well against the talented Austrians in Zurich; even without their bustling centre-forward Lawrie Reilly, Schmied in the Austrian goal had far more to do than did their own goalkeeper, Martin. And Mochan would have sent the game into extra-time for the Scots but for his brilliant save. As it was, Probst's first-half goal gave Austria their win. England threw away all the brilliant work of Matthews in a 4-4 draw with Belgium; they led 3-1 with only a quarter of an hour to go but two goals in five minutes from Anoul and Coppens sent the match into extra-time – where England got both further goals, though unfortunately one of them was an own goal by Jimmy Dickinson!

Meanwhile, the hosts Switzerland had upset all the form by beating Italy 2-1 in Lausanne. The Brazilian referee unfortunately allowed the match to degenerate into an orgy of fouls and bad temper. The Swiss got their winner twelve minutes from time but the win cost two of their team kicks in the stomach, and the referee was chased off the field by the Italians after he had disallowed a goal by the volatile Lorenzi.

The next round of matches produced one of the great 'ifs' of World Cup history. What would have happened *if* Werner Liebrich, the burly German centre-half, had not kicked Hungary's Puskas in their first meeting between the countries. It was arguably accidental but it put the Hungarian general out of the team until the Final – and he was still not fully fit then.

The match was also a master stroke of psychology by the German manager Herberger. He decided that, having beaten Turkey, they could afford to let the Hungarians win, and qualify by beating Turkey again in the play-off – which of course they duly did 7-2. But who could believe the scoreline of the match which turned out to be a rehearsal for the Final... Hungary 8 West Germany 3! The team of German reserves were torn apart, with Kocsis getting four goals and, despite Puskas' absence, Hungary piling it on at the end with three in

opposite **A strange Turkish wall presents no problem to Fritz Walter of West Germany, as he floats the ball over in the 4-1 win.**

left **A flying leap by the Mexican goalkeeper, but France won 3-2.**

above **The most famous of pre-war footballers, Stanley Matthews of England, was still skilful enough in 1954 to delight Swiss World Cup crowds with his dribbling.**

the last quarter of an hour.

In Group 1, the meeting of Brazil and Yugoslavia produced one of the games of the tournament. Zebec put Yugoslavia in front three minutes from half-time but, despite the agility of Beara in the Yugoslav goal, the Brazilian pressure eventually brought an equaliser when Didi lashed in a spectacular shot. Extra-time produced no more goals, so Brazil and Yugoslavia both went through.

Meanwhile, Scotland learned the hard facts of World Cup life in a seven-goal massacre by Uruguay in Basle, conceding five in the second half. Wingers Borges and Abbadie got five of the goals between them against a disorganised Scottish defence. The resignation of team manager Andy Beattie after the Austria game, following arguments with team officials, had obviously not helped the Scotland cause. So Austria were the other side to go safely through in this group, accounting for the Czechs 5-0 in Zurich with Probst getting three more goals.

In Group 4, England's 2-0 win against the totally inconsistent Swiss saw them through to the quarter-finals. It was a triumph for Wolverhampton Wanderers on a steaming hot day in Berne. Billy Wright had moved to centre-half in place of the injured Owen, team-mate Jimmy Mullen deputised for the injured Matthews and both he and his Wolves colleague Wilshaw scored.

Mercifully, the play-off between Switzerland and Italy did not produce the fireworks of the first encounter and the home side found sufficient dash and enthusiasm to brush aside the superior Italian technique in a 4-1 victory.

So to the quarter-finals, the sudden-death part of the tournament – and no let up in the welter of goals. In fact the four games averaged over six a piece! The closest of the four was West Germany's 2-0 win over Yugoslavia. Helmut Rahn, a massive raiding winger, recalled by Herberger from a successful tour he was making with his club in Uruguay, scored his first goal and underlined the threat of the full-strength Germans. Even so, the Yugoslavs were desperately unlucky to lose;

they dominated play for an hour until their towering defender Horvat sent a back-pass speeding into his own net. Full-back Kohlmeyer made three goal-line clearances for Germany before the burly Rahn burst clear to clinch the match with the second goal.

In Lausanne, on a boiling hot day, the passionate Swiss fans saw their team go out to Austria in one of the most amazing World Cup ties – a twelve-goal thriller! Switzerland raced into a three-goal lead but Austria, exploiting the speed of the Koerners on the wings and prompted, as ever, by the masterly Ocwirk, were undeterred. Their policy of shooting from long range brought them level in an incredible three-minute spell. They proceeded to add another two just before the Swiss pulled it back to 5-4, all before half-time! Wagner finished with three goals as Austria added two more in the second half. The Swiss star was the dark-haired inside forward Vonlanthen, who was behind most of the goals without scoring.

In Basle, England went out 4-2 to Uruguay but might have done better but for a 'nightmare' performance by goalkeeper Merrick. Even trailing 2-1, England had a chance to take command when Uruguay's 1950 captain Varela pulled a muscle shortly after scoring; the South Americans already had Andrade and Abbadie limping. But Merrick was too slow to reach Schiaffino's shot after Varela had taken a free kick by kicking the ball illegally as it dropped from his hands. Finney pulled it back to 3-2 and Matthews hit a post, but the Uruguayans survived and in a breakaway Ambrois clinched it with a fourth goal.

Which leaves just one quarter-final to report – the notorious 'Battle of Berne' between Hungary and Brazil. It was a match the English referee Arthur Ellis would remember all his life. There are those who say he saved an explosive situation from getting worse; others that one of his decisions was crucial. Either way, what could have been a great match degenerated into a disgraceful display of violence. It was

opposite above **Kocsis (behind No 9) scores one of his four goals in Hungary's 8-3 defeat of West Germany.**

left **Two England players, Tommy Taylor (10) and Dennis Wilshaw (15) beaten by Parlier, the Swiss goalkeeper, in the match won 2-0 by England.**

top **A Swiss player heads away in the extraordinary match between Austria and Switzerland – leading 5-4 at half-time, the Austrians won 7-5.**

above **The Hungarian team with its bouquet of flowers looks friendly enough – but this was just before the notorious 'Battle of Berne'.**

played in mud and driving rain, which obviously did not help tempers. But it was totally provocative when Hidegkuti scored for Hungary after four minutes for him to have his shorts ripped off him in the process, and the Hungarian Lorant showed an ominous contempt for the referee early on by laughing in his face after being cautioned for a bad foul. In the eighth minute Brazil were 2-0 down as Kocsis headed a second goal. Brazil's desperation increased and, with Hungary quite prepared to retaliate, the violence increased. Just before half-time, in fact, Buzansky bowled Indios over in the penalty area and Djalma Santos pulled it back to 2-1 from the penalty spot.

Hungary had Toth limping on the wing in the second half but there was no sign that they were missing Puskas, for whom Czibor deputised brilliantly. Then came a crucial decision. There was a mix-up in the Brazilian penalty area in which Kocsis collided with Djalma Santos and another

Brazilian defender fell to the ground, possibly touching the ball with his arm – and the melee ended with a penalty being awarded to Hungary, where both sides had expected a free kick to Brazil. Lantos took the kick and scored.

Julinho with a brilliant run and shot pulled it back to 3-2 . . . and then the real trouble started. Nilton Santos and Boszik came to blows and were sent off – but police had to intervene to see them off the pitch. Djalma Santos, at one point, chased Czibor all over the field before Humberto Tozzi, Brazil's inside forward, became the third player to be sent off, for kicking an opponent. He fell to his knees pleading with Arthur Ellis to let him stay – but in vain. A minute later Kocsis ('Golden Head', as they called him) lived up to his name with Hungary's fourth goal. The violence on the pitch led to 42 free kicks, 2 penalties, 4 cautions and 3 sending-offs, but the brawl did not end with the match. After the final whistle the enraged Brazilians turned out the lights in the players' tunnel and lay in wait for their opponents. They invaded the Hungarian dressing room, where fists and bottles and boots flew in the darkness, and there were several casualties. The one thing that came out of it from a Brazilian viewpoint was the decision taken by their football authorities to impose stricter discipline on their players. It was to pay off in later World Cup finals.

Happily, the Hungary v Uruguay semi-final was good enough to restore faith in the game itself. In fact, the match in Lausanne, which went to extra-time, is regarded as one of the finest in World Cup history. Hungary were still without Puskas; Uruguay were missing Varela, Abbadie and Miguez. It was 1-0 to Hungary at half-time, Czibor having volleyed in a header from the inevitable Kocsis. With only quarter of an hour left it was 2-0, Hidegkuti heading the second from Budai's cross. But then twice Schiaffino sent the Argentinian-born Hohberg through to score. So it went into extra-time. Hohberg could have completed an astonishing hat-trick but his shot hit a post. This and an injury to Schiaffino were too much for Uruguay and Kocsis won the match with two superb headers. So Uruguay went down 4-2, their first defeat in a World Cup match.

The other semi-final between West Germany and Austria was totally one-sided. Austria's goalkeeper Walter Zeman, who had replaced Schmied, had an awful game and the Germans won 6-1. Skipper Fritz Walter, who was in dazzling form, scored with two penalties, his brother Otmar scored two more from centre forward and Schaefer and Morlock got the others. Five of the goals came in the second half.

Austria had their consolation in the third place match. No one gave them a chance against the brilliant Uruguayans but the South Americans were jaded. Schiaffino was a passenger in the second half and Ocwirk inspired

opposite above **Didi, of Brazil, eludes Lantos of Hungary, while referee Arthur Ellis watches.**

left **Castilho, Brazil's goalkeeper, dives bravely to save at the feet of Sandor Kocsis, of Hungary.**

above **Inside-forward Morlock begins West Germany's fight-back in the 1954 Final by sliding the ball past the diving Grosics for their first goal.**

overleaf **Germany's equalizer, Rahn, who also got the winner, turns the ball past Grosics from a corner.**

Austria to a 3-1 win, scoring the last goal himself.

So to the Final in Berne, again played in heavy rain. Puskas was back, though not fully fit, and it was he who got the first goal after Kocsis' shot had been blocked. Two minutes later Czibor cut in from the right wing to make it 2-0 with only eight minutes gone.

The Germans were not demoralised, in fact their swift reply probably turned the match. Within three minutes Morlock had scored from Fritz Walter's centre and it was not long before Rahn thumped in the equaliser from a corner.

Turek's form in the German goal prevented Hungary taking control in the second half, but equally decisive were the Puskas' missed chances and the fact that both Hidegkuti and Kocsis hit the woodwork. Then, fifteen minutes from time, Fritz Walter's centre was only half cleared and Rahn smashed in a 15-yard shot. It was the match winner. But the final hammerblow for Hungary was when Puskas did at last find the net from Toth's fine diagonal pass only to have it disallowed for offside. Turek brought off a wonderful save from Czibor in the dying seconds and the cup went to Sepp Herberger's West Germany. The great Hungarian side had just failed to scale the final pinnacle. Within two years it was no more than a memory. That 8-3 win in the first round must have seemed like a bitter memory to Ferenc Puskas and his men. Not for the last time the more gifted team had lost a World Cup Final; twenty years later the West Germans were to give Holland a similar experience.

### 5th WORLD CUP Switzerland, 1954

**GROUP 1**
Yugoslavia (1)1 France (0)0
Milutinovic
Brazil (4)5 Mexico (0)0
Baltazar, Didi,
Pinga 2, Julinho
France (1)3 Mexico (0)2
Vincent, Cardenas   Naranjo, Balcazar
(og), Kopa (pen)
Brazil (0)(1)1 Yugoslavia (0)(1)1
Didi   Zebec

|  | P | W | D | L | F | A | Pts |
|---|---|---|---|---|---|---|---|
| Brazil | 2 | 1 | 1 | 0 | 6 | 1 | 3 |
| Yugoslavia | 2 | 1 | 1 | 0 | 2 | 1 | 3 |
| France | 2 | 1 | 0 | 1 | 3 | 3 | 2 |
| Mexico | 2 | 0 | 0 | 2 | 2 | 8 | 0 |

**GROUP 2**
Hungary (4)9 South Korea (0)0
Czibor, Kocsis 3,
Puskas 2, Lantos,
Palotas 2
West Germany (1)4 Turkey (1)1
Klodt, Morlock,   Suat
Schaefer, Walter (0)
Hungary (3)8 W. Germany (1)3
Hidegkuti 2, Kocsis 4,   Pfaff, Hermann,
Puskas, Toth   Rahn
Turkey (4)7 South Korea (0)0
Burhan 3, Erol,
Lefter, Suat 2

|  | P | W | D | L | F | A | Pts |
|---|---|---|---|---|---|---|---|
| Hungary | 2 | 2 | 0 | 0 | 17 | 3 | 4 |
| West Germany | 2 | 1 | 0 | 1 | 7 | 9 | 2 |
| Turkey | 2 | 1 | 0 | 1 | 8 | 4 | 2 |
| South Korea | 2 | 0 | 0 | 2 | 0 | 16 | 0 |

**Play-off**
West Germany (3)7 Turkey (1)2
Morlock 3, Walter (0),   Mustafa, Lefter
Walter (F), Schaefer 2

**GROUP 3**
Austria (1)1 Scotland (0)0
Probst
Uruguay (0)2 Czech. (0)0
Miguez, Schiaffino
Austria (4)5 Czech. (0)0
Stojaspal 2, Probst 3
Uruguay (2)7 Scotland (0)0
Borges 3, Miguez 2,
Abbadie 2

|  | P | W | D | L | F | A | Pts |
|---|---|---|---|---|---|---|---|
| Uruguay | 2 | 2 | 0 | 0 | 9 | 0 | 4 |
| Austria | 2 | 2 | 0 | 0 | 6 | 0 | 4 |
| Czechoslovakia | 2 | 0 | 0 | 2 | 0 | 7 | 0 |
| Scotland | 2 | 0 | 0 | 2 | 0 | 8 | 0 |

**GROUP 4**
England (2)(3)4 Belgium (1)(3)4
Broadis 2, Lofthouse 2   Anoul 2, Coppens,
  Dickinson (og)
Switzerland (1)2 Italy (1)1
Ballaman, Hugi   Boniperti
England (1)2 Switzerland (0)0
Mullen, Wilshaw
Italy (1)4 Belgium (0)1
Pandolfini (pen), Galli, Anoul
Frignani, Lorenzi

|  | P | W | D | L | F | A | Pts |
|---|---|---|---|---|---|---|---|
| England | 2 | 1 | 1 | 0 | 6 | 4 | 3 |
| Italy | 2 | 1 | 0 | 1 | 5 | 3 | 2 |
| Switzerland | 2 | 1 | 0 | 1 | 2 | 3 | 2 |
| Belgium | 2 | 0 | 1 | 1 | 5 | 8 | 1 |

**Play-off**
Switzerland (1)4 Italy (0)1
Hugi 2, Ballaman,   Nesti
Fatton

**QUARTER-FINALS**
West Germany (1)2 Yugoslavia (0)0
Horvat (og), Rahn
Hungary (2)4 Brazil (1)2
Hidegkuti 2, Kocsis,   Santos (D) (pen),
Lantos (pen)   Julinho
Austria (5)7 Switzerland (4)5
Koerner (A) 2,   Ballaman 2, Hugi 2,
Wagner 3, Probst   Hanappi (og)
Uruguay (2)4 England (1)2
Borges, Varela,   Lofthouse, Finney
Schiaffino, Ambrois

**SEMI-FINALS**
West Germany (1)6 Austria (0)1
Schaefer, Morlock,   Probst
Walter (F) 2 (2 pens),
Walter (0) 2
Hungary (1)(2)4 Uruguay (0)(2)2
Czibor, Hidegkuti,   Hohberg 2
Kocsis 2
**THIRD PLACE MATCH**: Zurich
Austria (1)3 Uruguay (1)1
Stojaspal (pen),   Hohberg
Cruz (og), Ocwirk

**FINAL**: Berne 4.7.54 Attendance 55,000
West Germany (2)3 Hungary (2)2
Morlock, Rahn 2   Puskas, Czibor
**West Germany**: Turek; Posipal,
Kohlmeyer, Eckel, Liebrich, Mai; Rahn,
Morlock, Walter (0), Walter (F) (capt),
Schaefer
**Hungary**: Grosics; Buzansky, Lantos,
Bozsik, Lorant, Zakarias; Czibor, Kocsis,
Hidegkuti, Puskas (capt), Toth (J)
**Referee**: Ling (England)

**LEADING SCORERS**
11—Kocsis (Hungary)
 6—Morlock (West Germany), Probst
    (Austria)
 5—Hugi (Switzerland)

# 1958 SWEDEN

FIFA membership: 86

Entries: 53

Finals: Four qualifying groups, quarter-finals onwards knock-out

Grounds: Malmo, Halmstad, Halsinborg, Norrkoping, Vasteras, Cerebro, Ekilstuna, Stockholm, Sandviken, Gothenburg, Boras

Leading scorer: Fontaine (France) 13 goals

Winners: Brazil

---

The 1958 finals in Sweden finished with the balance of world soccer power shifting away from Europe – and from the two nations which contested the Final so dramatically four years earlier. Hungary had been torn assunder by political upheaval and war. Of their 'wonderteam', four survivors went to Sweden – goalkeeper Grosics, wing-half Boszik, winger Budai and that deadly but now ageing centre-forward, Hidegkuti. But gone were their 'general' Ferenc Puskas, that incomparable header of the ball and scorer of eleven goals in the 1954 finals Sandor Kocsis, and winger Zoltan Czibor. They had all defected to the West. Kocsis and Czibor finished up with Barcelona, and Puskas helped to make Real Madrid the greatest club side in the world. The West Germans, still under Herberger, who was now assisted by his 'understudy' Helmut Schoen, were skippered by Fritz Walter and had two other survivors from Switzerland in 1954. Winger Schaefer had been converted into an inside forward and the burly Helmut Rahn had again been called into the front line. The new star was Horst Szymaniak, a muscular left-half. But the Germans were just short of the greatness necessary to hold onto their championship.

Missing entirely from the finals were two nations which had already won the title twice each. Uruguay had been thrashed out of their qualifying place 5-0 by unfancied Paraguay, while Northern Ireland, skippered by that cultured wing-half Danny Blanchflower and managed by Peter Doherty, had caused the other real qualifying upset by putting out the Italians. Sadly, Northern Ireland were without Danny Blanchflower's brother, centre-half Jackie – he had been in the Manchester United air disaster in Munich in February 1958. The same crash had torn the heart out of the England challenge by robbing them of full-back Roger Byrne, that prodigious young giant Duncan Edwards and centre-forward Tommy Taylor. They had all been instrumental in two significant England victories – 4-2 over Brazil at Wembley in 1956 and 3-1 the same year over the West Germans in Berlin.

Brazil had learned from that pretty disastrous European tour of 1956. They had a 4-2-4 formation and the makings of a side that could achieve real greatness. Milton Santos was still there. So, too, was Didi but it was to be the other inside forward that would capture the imagination of the world – a so far unknown seventeen-year-old called Pelé. The Argentinians, by comparison, were well short of the class that had won them the South American championship only the year before. Immediately after that success, the stars of the side had all been lured to Italy.

Scotland had eliminated Spain but were in mediocre form themselves, having been thrashed 4-0 in Glasgow by England. But Britain had four finalists because Wales, after Uruguay's withdrawal, were invited to play off for the last place against Israel, and that proved well within their capabilities. The Welsh were to rise to the occasion in surprising manner by putting out the Hungarians and conceding only one goal in their matches against both the eventual Finalists.

The side expected to do well – and they lived up to their odds – were the hosts, Sweden. Still under the guidance of George Raynor, the Yorkshireman who had taken them to third place in the 1950 finals, Sweden had at last recognised professionalism. This meant the recall from Italy of players like Gunnar Gren and Nils Liedholm, both members of the 1948 Olympic-winning side; Kurt Hamrin, a tricky outside right; 1950 World Cup hero Nacka Skoglund, the Inter Milan winger; and centre-half Julli Gustavsson. Round by round their threat was to grow, together of course with nationalistic support for them.

The home side opened the tournament in Stockholm with a comfortable enough win over Mexico. Agne Simonsson, a vigorous young centre-forward, got two of the goals, while Liedholm scored the other one from the penalty spot. To underline Raynor's gamble on experience, Bror Mellberg, another member of the 1950 World Cup side, was at inside right.

In the same group, Hungary struggled to a 1-1 draw with the rejuvenated Welsh. Indeed, Hungary's goal was attributable to the fact that Jack Kelsey, the Welsh goalkeeper, who was one of the outstanding individuals in the whole tournament, was dazzled by the sun as Boszik went through in the fourth minute. The equaliser came from the head of the giant John Charles, another player recalled from Italy for the finals.

England found herself in the toughest qualifying pool of all, against Russia, Brazil and Austria. The Russians had won the Olympic tournament in Melbourne

33

in 1956 and in Lev Yashin they had one of the finest goalkeepers in the history of the game. The England v Russia match in Gothenburg turned out to be an exciting 2-2 draw, with England needing a real fightback to save the game after trailing 2-0, and this despite the fact that Russia played without their fine captain and left-half, Netto. A ruthless tackle put England winger Tom Finney out of the tournament but not before he had equalised with a penalty. In the same group, Brazil beat Austria 3-0 in Boras. Pelé was injured and did not play. In his absence two of the goals fell to nineteen-year-old Jose 'Mazzola' Altafini, already signed expensively by Inter-Milan.

Argentina went down 3-1 to a more efficient West German side. They had no answer to Rahn, who added two more to his tally of World Cup goals. The brave Irish started splendidly in Halmstadt with a 1-0 win over the Czechs; Harry Gregg kept alive the British reputation for producing fine goalkeepers and the tough little Wilbur Cush got the vital goal.

In Group 2, France surprised even themselves with an astonishing 7-2 massacre of Paraguay. Manager Paul Nicholas had bred tremendous understanding and morale during the weeks in a training camp at Kopparberg, and they had an outstanding inside forward trio in Raymond Kopa,

opposite, far left **Sweden's ancient warriors, who did so well in the 1958 finals, being presented to King Gustav Adolf before the start of their first match in Stockholm.**

left **Lev Yashin, one of the most popular of Russian footballers, kept goal in the 1958 World Cup.**

opposite below **Holders West Germany got off to a good start with a 3-1 win over Argentina. Labruna and Stollenwerk tussle for the ball.**

below **England's best performance in 1958 was a 0-0 draw with eventual winners Brazil. England goalkeeper Colin McDonald, who was superb, catches a high ball.**

back from Real Madrid, Biantoni and Juste Fontaine, a player who expected to be reserve but finished the championship as top scorer. He started with a hat-trick against Paraguay. Scotland, meanwhile, undeterred by England's 5-0 defeat in Yugoslavia on their way to Sweden, held the Slavs to a good 1-1 draw in Vasteras. Petakovic scored in seven minutes for Yugoslavia but Murray earned Scotland her point.

England's best performance was in holding Brazil to a goalless draw in her second match. Bill Nicholson, the Spurs coach and assistant to manager Walter Winterbottom, had worked out a tactical plan to counter Brazil's 4-2-4 system. Don Howe moved from right-back to the middle, Eddie Clamp played the role of an attacking right-back and the other wing-half, Bill Slater, marked Didi out of the game. The defence took all the honours, with goalkeeper Colin McDonald outstanding. It was the only time Brazil failed to score. England's one flash of hope was when Kevan was felled by Bellini for what looked a certain penalty. Remember, though, Pelé, Zito and the wily winger Garrincha were waiting in the wings.

Meanwhile, Austria now succumbed 2-0 to Russia in Boras and Argentina recalled forty-year-old Angel Labruna at inside left to give Northern Ireland an unexpected 3-1 shock in Halmstad. There was something of a shock, too, for the Germans in Halsin-

opposite above **Harry Gregg kept goal brilliantly for Northern Ireland in their best-ever World Cup tournament, but could not stop this shot by Uwe Seeler in a 2-2 draw with West Germany.**

opposite, far left **John Charles, right, played superbly for Wales. In this match against Czechoslovakia he is tackling Bubnik.**

left **Johnny Haynes of England and Lev Yashin of Russia go for the ball in Russia's 1-0 win in a play-off for the quarter final.**

Above **Wales went out 1-0 in the quarter-final to Brazil. Ivor Allchurch of Wales rises above Bellini and Di Sordi to get in his header.**

borg, where Czechoslovakia took them all the way in a 2-2 draw. Rahn scored again and Schaefer got the other one.

Group 2 produced two more surprises with the 3-2 wins for Paraguay over Scotland and Yugoslavia against France. Scotland looked a jaded side and, well as centre-half Bobby Evans played, Paraguay's centre-forward Parodi proved the match winner. Yugoslavia's win over France was a travesty of justice, with the winning goal coming in a breakaway three minutes from time.

Wales, after the excellent 1-1 draw with Hungary, would have expected better than a repeat against the unfancied Mexicans. The following day, the Swedes took another step towards the place in the Final that manager Raynor predicted by beating Hungary 2-1. Hamrin got both the Swedish goals and Hungary's chance went with the disallowing of Tichy's shot which cannoned down off the crossbar in the fifty-fifth minute.

Northern Ireland earned a very creditable draw with West Germany in Malmo, thanks to superb goalkeeping again by Gregg and two goals from Peter McParland. This meant the Irish playing-off with Czechoslovakia, who finished with an astonishing 6-1 rout of a leaden-footed Argentina.

England and Wales were also involved in play-offs, thanks to drawing their final matches. Wales were given an easy ride in a 0-0 game against a side of Swedish reserves, while England were held 2-2 by the plodding Austrians.

The other British team, Scotland, went out after a 2-1 defeat by France in Cerebro with goals by Kopa and Fontaine. Wales raised themselves to new heights to win the play-off with Hungary 2-1 in Stockholm. It was a rough game with Sipos of Hungary sent off. Tichy scored first for Hungary, Ivor Allchurch equalised with a superb forty-yard volley and Terry Medwin got a cheeky winning goal when he intercepted a short goal kick by goalkeeper Grosics.

top The semi-final, and Vava of Brazil blasts the ball past the French goalkeeper from close range.

above Just Fontaine in 1967, after being made manager of the French football team. In 1958 he scored 13 goals for France in the World Cup finals, a record.

top right The 1958 Final, and after four minutes Liedholm puts Sweden a goal up.

right The 17-year-old Pelé came to the notice of the world in the 1958 Final. Here the Swedish goalkeeper Kalle Svensson manages to punch clear from his head.

opposite above Vicente Feola, the Brazilian trainer, kisses the Jules Rimet trophy – the first of Brazil's wins.

opposite below Winners Brazil did a lap of honour round the ground carrying the flag of host nation Sweden after their brilliant victory.

Northern Ireland equally made history with their 2-1 win after extra-time against the Czechs. The Irish survived injuries to goalkeeper Uprichard and wing-half Peacock, and the handicap of going a goal behind; McParland again scored both their goals. England were unlucky against the Russians; winger Brabrook twice hit the post before Russia's Ilyin shot the winner, ironically in-off a post.

When it came to the quarter-finals, the Irish had run out of steam and players. After a superfluous coach trip they crashed 4-0 to the French at Norrkoping. Inside forward Casey had to play with four stitches in a shin and goalkeeper Gregg had a damaged leg. Wales, meanwhile, put up a superb show against Brazil.

They were without the giant John Charles, but his brother Mel played courageously at centre-half and Hopkins contained Garrincha. In the end they only fell to a solitary goal by Pelé which was deflected past goalkeeper Kelsey – a personal tragedy for him after a brilliant performance; Pelé has called it 'the most important goal of my career'.

Sweden beat Russia comfortably 2-0 with a goal and a masterly performance from Hamrin. And in the other quarter-final, Yugoslavia had most of the game against West Germany in Malmo and then fell to a goal by Rahn. So to the semi-finals. Brazil v France in Stockholm and Sweden v West Germany in Gothenburg.

The Swedes now had a nation behind them. The title was only two matches away. The Swedish cheer leaders roused the Gothenburg crowd; the German ones were banned from the running track! But the Germans were undeterred on the pitch. Uwe Seeler, their new centre-forward, crossed the ball and inside left Schaefer volleyed a brilliant goal against the run of play. Five minutes later, Sweden were level. Liedholm certainly handled in the build-up to the goal, which was shot home from a sharp angle by Skoglund. Three minutes after half-time came a turning point, with the score still 1-1. German full-back Juskowiak lashed out at the elusive Hamrin and was sent off. The Germans suffered a further setback when Parling got away with a dreadful foul on Fritz Walter, which left the German skipper hobbling. The balance swung towards Sweden and, nine minutes from time, Gren put them ahead. Just to make sure, Hamrin crowned a superb performance with a cheeky individual goal.

In the other semi-final, France ran out of luck. After thirty-seven minutes their elegant centre-half Bob Jonquet was injured and their whole defence was wrecked. At that stage it was 1-1. Vava had put Brazil ahead in two minutes and Fontaine had equalised. But the second half was a slaughter. Didi restored Brazil's lead with a swerving, long-range shot and then masterminded a hat-trick for the precocious Pelé. Pianton's late goal for France was cold comfort to them – the final score was 5-2 to Brazil. At least the French took third place with an emphatic 6-3 win over Germany and four more goals for Fontaine. His record total of thirteen for the tournament still stands.

The Swedish manager George Raynor gave his side their biggest chance of victory in the Final if they scored first. The Brazilians, he forecast, would 'panic all over the show'. But it didn't work out that way. Liedholm did indeed thread his way through to put Sweden ahead in only four minutes but Brazil were not upset. By half-time, the swooping Garrincha had twice hurtled through the Swedish defence to lay on goals for Vava. And in the second half, Brazil were irresistible. Pelé juggled one astonishing goal and headed another and, in between, left winger Zagalo, later to manage Brazil, got the other one.

The best team had won and a man later to become a football legend had begun his chequered World Cup career in storybook fashion.

A plate commemorating Brazil's 1958 win in the Maracana Stadium.

### 6th WORLD CUP Sweden, 1958

**GROUP 1**
West Germany (2)3 Argentina (1)1
Rahn 2, Schmidt    Corbatta
N. Ireland (1)1 Czech. (0)0
Cush
West Germany (1)2 Czech. (0)2
Schaefer, Rahn    Dvorak (pen), Zikan
Argentina (1)3 N. Ireland (1)1
Corbatta 2 (1 pen)    McParland
Menendez
West Germany (1)2 N. Ireland (1)2
Rahn, Seeler    McParland 2
Czechoslovakia (3)6 Argentina (1)1
Dvorak, Zikan 2,    Corbatta
Feureisl, Hovorka 2

|               | P | W | D | L | F | A | Pts |
|---------------|---|---|---|---|---|---|-----|
| West Germany  | 3 | 1 | 2 | 0 | 7 | 5 | 4   |
| Czechoslovakia| 3 | 1 | 1 | 1 | 8 | 4 | 3   |
| N. Ireland    | 3 | 1 | 1 | 1 | 4 | 5 | 3   |
| Argentina     | 3 | 1 | 0 | 2 | 5 | 10| 2   |

Play-off
N. Ireland (1)(1)2 Czecho. (1)(1)1
McParland 2    Zikan

**GROUP 2**
France (2)7 Paraguay (2)3
Fontaine 3, Piantoni,    Amarilla 2 (1 pen),
Kopa, Wisnieski,    Romero
Vincent
Yugoslavia (1)1 Scotland (0)1
Petakovic    Murray
Yugoslavia (1)3 France (1)2
Petakovic,    Fontaine 2
Veselinovic 2

Paraguay (2)3 Scotland (1)2
Aguero, Re, Parodi    Mudie, Collins
France (2)2 Scotland (0)1
Kopa, Fontaine    Baird
Yugoslavia (2)3 Paraguay (1)3
Ognjanovic, Rajkov,    Parodi, Aguero,
Veselinovic    Romero

|            | P | W | D | L | F  | A  | Pts |
|------------|---|---|---|---|----|----|-----|
| France     | 3 | 2 | 0 | 1 | 11 | 7  | 4   |
| Yugoslavia | 3 | 1 | 2 | 0 | 7  | 6  | 4   |
| Paraguay   | 3 | 1 | 1 | 1 | 9  | 12 | 3   |
| Scotland   | 3 | 0 | 1 | 2 | 4  | 6  | 1   |

**GROUP 3**
Sweden (1)3 Mexico (0)0
Simonsson 2,
Liedholm (pen)
Hungary (1)1 Wales (1)1
Bozsik    Charles (J)
Wales (1)1 Mexico (1)1
Allchurch    Belmonte
Sweden (1)2 Hungary (0)1
Hamrin 2    Tichy
Hungary (1)4 Mexico (0)0
Tichy 2, Sandor,
Bencsics
Sweden (0)0 Wales (0)0

|         | P | W | D | L | F | A | Pts |
|---------|---|---|---|---|---|---|-----|
| Sweden  | 3 | 2 | 1 | 0 | 5 | 1 | 5   |
| Hungary | 3 | 1 | 1 | 1 | 6 | 3 | 3   |
| Wales   | 3 | 0 | 3 | 0 | 2 | 2 | 3   |
| Mexico  | 3 | 0 | 1 | 2 | 1 | 8 | 1   |

Play-off
Wales (0)2 Hungary (1)1
Allchurch, Medwin    Tichy

**GROUP 4**
England (0)2 USSR (1)2
Kevan, Finney (pen)    Simonian,
                       Ivanov (A)
Brazil (1)3 Austria (0)0
Mazzola 2, Santos (N)
England (0)0 Brazil (0)0
USSR (1)2 Austria (0)0
Ilyin, Ivanov (V)
Brazil (1)2 USSR (0)0
Vava 2
England (0)2 Austria (1)2
Haynes, Kevan    Koller, Koerner

|         | P | W | D | L | F | A | Pts |
|---------|---|---|---|---|---|---|-----|
| Brazil  | 3 | 2 | 1 | 0 | 5 | 0 | 5   |
| England | 3 | 0 | 3 | 0 | 4 | 4 | 3   |
| USSR    | 3 | 1 | 1 | 1 | 4 | 4 | 3   |
| Austria | 3 | 0 | 1 | 2 | 2 | 7 | 1   |

Play-off
USSR (0)1 England (0)0
Ilyin

**QUARTER-FINALS**
France (1)4 N. Ireland (0)0
Wisnieski, Fontaine 2,
Piantoni
West Germany (1)1 Yugoslavia (0)0
Rahn

Sweden (0)2 USSR (0)0
Hamrin, Simonsson
Brazil (0)1 Wales (0)0
Pele

**SEMI-FINALS**
Brazil (2)5 France (1)2
Veva, Didi, Pele 3    Fontaine, Piantoni
Sweden (1)3 W. Germany (1)1
Skoglund, Gren    Schaefer
Hamrin

**THIRD PLACE MATCH**: Gothenburg
France (0)6 W. Germany (0)3
Fontaine 4, Kopa (pen)    Cieslarczyk, Rahn,
Douis    Schaefer

**FINAL**: Stockholm 29.6.58
Attendance 49,737
Brazil (2)5 Sweden (1)2
Vava 2, Pele 2,    Liedholm,
Zagalo    Simonsson
**Brazil**: Gylmar; Santos (D), Santos (N); Zito, Bellini, Orlando; Garrincha, Didi, Vava, Pete, Zagalo
**Sweden**: Svensson; Bergmark, Axbom; Boerjesson, Gustavsson, Parling; Hamrin, Gren, Simonsson, Liedholm, Skoglund
**Referee**: Guigue (France)

**LEADING SCORERS**
13—Fontaine (France)
7—Rahn (West Germany)
6—Pele (Brazil)

40

# 1962 CHILE

FIFA membership: 104

Entrants: 57

Finals: Four qualifying groups, goal average to decide ties, not play-offs; quarter-final onwards, knock-out

Grounds: Arica, Santiago, Vina del Mar, Rancagua

Leading scorers: Albert (Hungary), Ivanov (Russia), Sanchez (Chile), Garrincha (Brazil), Jerkovic (Yugoslavia), Vava (Brazil) 4 goals

Winners: Brazil

Controversially, and ultimately compassionately, the 1962 World Cup finals were given to Chile because rather than despite the fact that the country had only recently been devastated by earthquakes. However, despite her economic problem, the Chileans managed to build a fine new national stadium in Santiago, and generally made a pretty good job of the organisation apart from charging astronomical admission prices.

As a tournament it never reached great heights. So many of the qualifying games were dominated by defences–only four of the thirty-two matches produced more than four goals, and seven produced one or less; six players shared the goalscoring honours with a mere four goals apiece.

Clearly the South American assault would be formidable with five finalists. Brazil, the holders, brought the nucleus of the side that had won in Sweden, although the gifted Pelé survived only one complete game. Chile, with the nation behind her, would surprise everyone. So indeed would little Colombia.

Of the European finalists, Italy and Spain brought with them a liberal helping of South American stars. Italy had Altafini from the 1958 Brazilian side plus the Argentinian Sivori. Spain brought Santamaria from the Uruguayan World Cup side of 1954 as well as Real Madrid's most valuable imports, Ferenc Puskas, star of the 1954 Hungarians, and that supreme Argentinian, di Stefano. However, di Stefano never actually played, protesting injury but apparently having fallen out with team manager Helenio Herrera. The Eastern European line-up was formidable. Russia was strongly tipped to push the holders Brazil the hardest; they had beaten Argentina, Uruguay and Chile on their recent South American tour. Otherwise, the line-up was pretty mediocre. England–the only British representative this time–had lost to Scotland in Glasgow for the first time in twenty-five years. Hungary were still in decline. Herberger had Germany as organised as ever but they lacked the leadership of a Fritz Walter. And, on paper, all that Chile had was home support.

Brazil, playing their matches in the beautiful seaside resort of Vina del Mar, were up against the polyglot Spaniards, the Czechs with their celebrated half-back line of Pluskal, Popluhar and the gifted Josef Masopust, and the unpredictable Mexicans.

Brazil opened with a 2-0 win over Mexico with goals from Zagalo and Pelé. But in their next match a goalless draw with the Czechs, the champions lost Pelé with a severely pulled muscle. It was the end of the tournament for him. Spain gave Brazil a shock in their next match. Hererra's re-organised, young side actually led 1-0 at half-time through Adelardo but in the second half the sheer brilliance of Garrincha tipped the scales Brazil's way by providing two goals for Pelé's twenty-four-year-old replacement, Amarildo. The Brazilians had Vava and Didi back from Madrid, and Mauro, Bellini's deputy in Sweden, had

**Spanish players Amancio, Suarez and Reifa prepare in Madrid for the 1962 World Cup finals.**

above **Amarildo** replaced the injured Pele for the match against Spain and his two second-half goals which won the match led to emotional congratulations from officials.

right The Italy-Chile match contained some ugly scenes. Three Italian players attempt to help team-mate Maschio, whose nose was broken by a well-televised left-hook from a Chilean.

far right **Lev Yashin** had a disastrous game against Columbia and nearly lost Russia the match.

taken over at centre-half. Zagalo dropped further back after Pelé's injury but the star of the side was the ungainly looking Garrincha. One leg shorter than the other, this lop-sided looking little character had incredible pace and swerve as well as deadly finishing power with boot and head. So Brazil dropped only one point in the draw with the Czechs, who accompanied them into the quarter-finals thanks to a 1-0 win over Spain.

In Group 2, in which Chile lined up with West Germany, Italy and Switzerland, everything was overshadowed by the disgraceful brawl which soured the Chile-Italy match. The trouble had been inflamed before the game by articles written by Italian journalists criticising life in Chile, and the home side's physical style did not help. The Italians inevitably retaliated and, as a result, had two players, full-back David and inside left Ferrini, sent off. Their inside right Maschio suffered a broken nose thanks to a famous left hook which was witnessed by everyone except English referee Ken Aston. Eventually, and almost incidentally, two second-half goals gave Chile the match. They went down by the same score, however, to the Germans thanks to a breakaway goal by Seeler and Szymaniak's penalty. The Germans, after starting with a goal-less match against Italy, had already beaten Switzerland 2-1, so this win saw them through. Chile were already through, so Italy's final 3-0 win over the Swiss was meaningless.

Far up in the north, at Arica, Russia were the disappointment, Colombia the surprise. First the Colombians gave Uruguay a scare before Uruguay scraped through 2-1 after being behind at half-time. Then they shocked the mighty Russians. On this rare occasion, goalkeeper Yashin was not at his best. By midway through the first half Russia led 3-0; it appeared to be all over. Colombia pulled one back before half-time but a further Russian goal seemed to put the issue beyond doubt. Then Yashin's poise went. He let in a goal direct from a corner kick. Two more Colombian goals followed and in the end the Russian goalkeeper had to save them from the ignominy of what would have been an unbelievable defeat. Nevertheless, Russia topped the group, going through with Yugoslavia. And these two sides met in another of the tournament's most brutal matches. The really incredible feature of it was that no one was sent off. Dubinski, the Russian full-back, had his leg broken by Mujic, who was promptly sent home by the manager. And how Yugoslavia's Jerkovic stayed on the pitch after aiming a blow at the referee no one knew. Happily, skill shone through and, with Yashin keeping the Yugoslavs at bay, Ponedelnik was able to engineer the two goals that gave Russia victory. First, his free kick hit the bar for Ivanov to score and then he added the second himself. Both Russia and Yugoslavia beat Uruguay and, in the final match, the Colombians had clearly shot their bolt, for they crashed 5-0 to the Slavs.

The Group 4 matches were played at Rancagua between Argentina, Bulgaria, England and Hungary.

43

The Argentinians opened with a tough 1-0 win over Bulgaria with a goal from right winger Facundo. Then the Hungarians beat England 2-1. It was an England performance that did not suggest that vast strides had been made since the disastrous encounters with Puskas and company five years before. A new wing-half called Bobby Moore had just come into the England team. But even with the skill and pace of wingers Bryan Douglas and Bobby Charlton and the midfield skill of Haynes it was not enough. Tichy left Springett in the England goal stranded with a long-range shot. Flowers equalised from a penalty and then Florian Albert, a superbly talented centre-forward, won the match for Hungary with a flash of individual brilliance.

England made a much better showing against Argentina. Flowers gave them the lead with another penalty, Charlton scored the second and that mercurial little inside forward Jimmy Greaves got a third. Argentina's

left **Gerry Hitchens robustly challenges Hungarian goalkeeper Grosics in England's first match, which Hungary won 2-1.**

below **The 1962 Final and Zito shows his joy at putting Brazil in the lead against Czechoslovakia.**

only goal came from a miskick by Sanfilippo. The Hungarians then thrashed the Bulgarians 6-1 with three more goals for Albert and finished off with a goalless draw with Argentina. England also finished with a goalless draw – against Bulgaria. This gave them the second qualifying place behind Hungary on the newly introduced system of goal average.

In their quarter-final, England faced Brazil in Vina del Mar, and, but for an unhappy performance by the England goalkeeper Springett, it could have been a lot closer than the final 3-1 margin to the holders. The irrepressible Garrincha was Brazil's match winner. First he outjumped the towering centre-half Maurice Norman to head the opening goal from a corner. England equalised through Gerry Hitchens, the centre-forward from Inter Milan who was replacing the injured Peacock. And so it stayed into the second half, until the unlucky Springett could not hold a swerving Garrincha free kick and Vava scored. Garrincha himself scored again with a long shot for the third.

In Santiago, Yugoslavia had revenge over West Germany for their defeat in the 1958 quarter-finals. Dragoslav Sekularac was again their star, along with Radakovic, the right-half, who scored the only goal of the game four minutes from time despite the handicap of playing with a bandaged head.

In Arica, the Chileans generated more nationalistic fervour by disposing of the Russians 2-1. Yashin had his second poor game. He was deceived by Leonel Sanchez's free kick after ten minutes and then was completely beaten by Eladio Rojas' 35-yard shot for the second. Chislenko pulled one back for the Russians almost immediately but Chile held out.

The other quarter-final in Rancagua continued the run of outsiders Czechoslovakia. So far their only win had been 1-0 against Spain, albeit a side packed with talent like Gento, Suarez, Puskas and Del Sol. Now they saw off the Hungarians, thanks mainly to goalkeeper Schroiff, a little luck from the posts and a breakaway goal from inside right Scherer after thirteen minutes. Tichy had an equaliser disallowed for offside.

In the semi-final at Santiago, the chips were down for Chile at last. They must meet Brazil. And, despite their massive support, the Chileans had the same trouble as England – they could not hold Garrincha. After nine minutes a magnificent 20-yard shot from him put Brazil ahead. He then headed the second from a corner. Toro pulled one back for Chile with a mighty free kick but, soon after half-time, Vava headed home a Garrincha corner. Sanchez made it 3-2 with a Chilean penalty but Vava's head settled it beyond doubt from Zagalo's centre.

Meanwhile, in Vina del Mar, the 'dark horses' still kept going. The nation's gaze was on Santiago and the match with Brazil, so a mere 5,000 spectators saw Czechoslovakia put out Yugoslavia 3-1. Goalkeeper Schroiff was again the hero for the Czechs who, nonetheless, well deserved their win. Kadraba gave them the lead after a goalless first half and, try as they might, the Slavs could turn their domination into no more than an equaliser from Jerkovic. A breakaway by Scherer put the Czechs back in front and a stupid handling offence by Markovic gave Scherer and the jubilant Czechs the match at 3-1 and a surprise place in the Final... their first since 1934.

Czechoslovakia were not overawed by the champions in the Final. They gave Brazil an early shock. Scherer glided a diagonal ball through the Brazilian defence and Masopust finished off a superb move. Sadly for the Czechs, goalkeeper Schroiff had run out of good games. He should have cut out Amarildo's equaliser from the narrowest of angles; he could do nothing about the second. Amarildo completely turned the Czech defence and Zito hurtled in to head home his centre. Thirteen minutes from the end, Djalma Santos hoisted a lob into the Czech goalmouth, Schroiff 'lost' it in the blinding sun and Vava had a simple task to score number three. It was poor reward for the midfield skill and energy of Kvasniak, who did so much for the losers. But Brazil, even without Pelé, and with experience rather than pace now their hallmark, were still too good for the best Europe could offer.

The victorious Brazilians of 1962. The players are, left to right, back: Djalma Santos, Zito, Gilmar, Zozimo, Nilton Santos, Mauro. Front: Masajista (masseur), Garrincha, Didi, Vava, Amarildo, Zagalo.

### 7th WORLD CUP Chile, 1962

**GROUP 1**
Uruguay (0)2 Colombia (1)1
  Cubilla, Sasia   Zaluaga
USSR (0)2 Yugoslavia (0)0
  Ivanov, Ponedelnik
Yugoslavia (2)3 Uruguay (1)1
  Skoblar, Galic,   Cabrera
  Jerkovic
USSR (3)4 Columbia (1)4
  Ivanov 2, Chislenko,   Aceros, Coll, Rada,
  Ponedelnik   Klinger
USSR (1)2 Uruguay (0)1
  Mamikin, Ivanov   Sasia
Yugoslavia (2)5 Colombia (0)0
  Galic, Jerkovic 3,
  Melic

| | P | W | D | L | F | A | Pts |
|---|---|---|---|---|---|---|---|
| USSR | 3 | 2 | 1 | 0 | 8 | 5 | 5 |
| Yugoslavia | 3 | 2 | 0 | 1 | 8 | 3 | 4 |
| Uruguay | 3 | 1 | 0 | 2 | 4 | 6 | 2 |
| Colombia | 3 | 0 | 1 | 2 | 5 | 11 | 1 |

**GROUP 2**
Chile (1)3 Switzerland (1)1
  Sanchez (L) 2,   Wuthrich
  Ramirez
West Germany (0)0 Italy (0)0
Chile (0)2 Italy (0)0
  Ramirez, Toro

West Germany (1)2 Switzerland (1)1
  Brulls, Seeler   Schneiter
West Germany (1)2 Chile (0)0
  Szymaniak (pen),
  Seeler
Italy (1)3 Switzerland (0)0
  Mora, Bulgarelli 2

| | P | W | D | L | F | A | Pts |
|---|---|---|---|---|---|---|---|
| West Germany | 3 | 2 | 1 | 0 | 4 | 1 | 5 |
| Chile | 3 | 2 | 0 | 1 | 5 | 3 | 4 |
| Italy | 3 | 1 | 1 | 1 | 3 | 2 | 3 |
| Switzerland | 3 | 0 | 0 | 3 | 2 | 8 | 0 |

**GROUP 3**
Brazil (0)2 Mexico (0)0
  Zagalo, Pele
Czechoslovakia (0)1 Spain (0)0
  Stibranyi
Brazil (0)0 Czech. (0)0
Spain (0)1 Mexico (0)0
  Peiro
Brazil (0)2 Spain (1)1
  Amarildo 2   Adelardo
Mexico (2)3 Czech. (1)1
  Diaz, Del Aguila,   Masek
  Hernandez (H) (pen)

| | P | W | D | L | F | A | Pts |
|---|---|---|---|---|---|---|---|
| Brazil | 3 | 2 | 1 | 0 | 4 | 1 | 5 |
| Czechoslovakia | 3 | 1 | 1 | 1 | 2 | 3 | 3 |
| Mexico | 3 | 1 | 0 | 2 | 3 | 4 | 2 |
| Spain | 3 | 1 | 0 | 2 | 2 | 3 | 2 |

**GROUP 4**
Argentina (1)1 Bulgaria (0)0
  Facundo
Hungary (1)2 England (0)1
  Tichy, Albert   Flowers (pen)
England (2)3 Argentina (0)1
  Flowers (pen),   Sanfilippo
  Charlton, Greaves
Hungary (4)6 Bulgaria (0)1
  Albert 3, Tichy 2,   Sokolov
  Solymosi
Argentina (0)0 Hungary (0)0
England (0)0 Bulgaria (0)0

| | P | W | D | L | F | A | Pts |
|---|---|---|---|---|---|---|---|
| Hungary | 3 | 2 | 1 | 0 | 8 | 2 | 5 |
| England | 3 | 1 | 1 | 1 | 4 | 3 | 3 |
| Argentina | 3 | 1 | 1 | 1 | 2 | 3 | 3 |
| Bulgaria | 3 | 0 | 1 | 2 | 1 | 7 | 1 |

**QUARTER-FINALS**
Yugoslavia (1)1 W. Germany (0)0
  Radakovic
Brazil (1)3 England (1)1
  Garrincha 2, Vava   Hitchens

Chile (2)2 USSR (1)1
  Sanchez (L), Rojas   Chislenko
Czechoslovakia (1)1 Hungary (0)0
  Scherer

**SEMI-FINALS**
Brazil (2)4 Chile (1)2
  Garrincha 2, Vava 2   Toro, Sanchez (L)
    (pen)
Czechoslovakia (0)3 Yugoslavia (0)1
  Kadraba, Scherer 2   Jerkovic
  (1 pen)

**THIRD PLACE MATCH:** Santiago
Chile (0)1 Yugoslavia (0)0
  Rojas

**FINAL:** Santiago 17.6.62
Attendance 69,068
Brazil (1)3 Czech. (1)1
  Amarildo, Zito, Vava   Masopust
**Barzil:** Gylmar; Santos (D), Santos (N); Zito, Mauro, Zozimo; Garrincha, Didi, Vava, Amarildo, Zagalo.
**Czechoslovakia:** Schroiff; Tichy, Novak; Pluskal, Popluhar, Masopust; Pospichal, Scherer, Kvasnak, Kadraba, Jelinek
**Referee:** Latychev (USSR)
**LEADING SCORERS:**
4—Albert (Hungary), Ivanov (USSR), Sanchez (Chile), Garrincha (Brazil), Jerkovic (Yugoslavia), Vava (Brazil)

# 1966 ENGLAND

FIFA membership: 125

Entries: 71

Finals: Four qualifying groups; quarter-finals onwards, knock-out

Grounds: Wembley; White City; Hillsborough, Sheffield; Villa Park, Birmingham; Goodison Park, Liverpool; Old Trafford, Manchester; Middlesbrough; Sunderland

Leading scorer: Eusebio 9 goals

Winners: England

---

On February 27, 1963, England swept away the cobwebs of the amateur age, and appointed Alf Ramsey as national team manager. He was a professional. An international player with thirty-two caps, he had known the ignominy of losing to the United States in the World Cup of 1950, and had digested at first hand the lessons of the 1953 Hungarians. He resented competing on unequal terms with anyone. England, he knew, could never rival the top Europeans or the South Americans while the team was selected by, and to a large extent run by, the amateurs of the International Selection Committee. He insisted on – and got – full control.

left The draw for the 1966 World Cup at the Royal Garden Hotel, London, took place before a battery of delegates, reporters, photographers and television cameras.

below Two of the grounds for the 1966 finals, Wembly Stadium, for the London group, and Old Trafford, Manchester, for the North-West group.

47

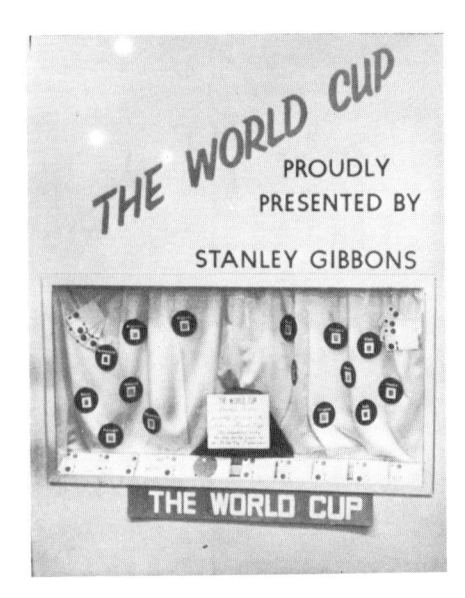

above **A 1966 pre-World Cup sensation was the theft of the trophy itself. Stanley Gibbons, the stamp dealers, proudly presented it at a stamp exhibition, and a thief took them at their word. All was well eight days later when a dog called Pickles found the Cup undamaged in his garden. His proud owner collected the reward.**

opposite, above left **Bobby Charlton scored one of his 'specials' against Mexico to start England on their trail to final victory.**

opposite, above right **Bulgaria's best footballer Gundi Asparoukhov, later killed in an accident.**

opposite below **Alcindo of Brazil, jumps a defender and cracks for goal against Bulgaria. Goalkeeper Naidenov is well beaten, but the shot was just wide.**

The Committee men were reduced to what Ramsey regarded as their true level of the cocktail party circuit, and English football was lifted back into world class. The new England boss, rarely given to flamboyant outbursts or predictions, had no illusions about his target. 'We shall win the World Cup', he said. He had home advantage to help him do it; three truly World class players as the core of his side; and just as important, a system. To some, 4-3-3, as his formation was called, was anathema. 'Ramsey's wingless wonders', they mocked. But it won a World Cup and bred a tactical revolution which has survived for more than a decade right across the world of football.

The 1966 World Cup was the tournament of Brazil's surprising downfall. The world champions, with their 1958 manager Vincent Feola in charge again, built a side around veterans like Orlando, Bellini, Djalma Santos and Garrincha. As for Pelé, he would last only two matches, ruthlessly kicked out of the competition. It was a tournament where organisation counted for more than individual brilliance. The superbly gifted Hungarians, for example, suffered from poor goalkeeping. The elegant, athletic Portuguese would probably have won with a defence to match their brilliant attack. In Eusebio, the African star from Benfica, Portugal had not only the top goalscorer with nine but probably the outstanding player of the tournament. No, there was not much for the uncommitted to get excited about, unless it was the fiction-like form of the totally anonymous men from North Korea with the unpronounceable names who knocked out mighty Italy and gave Portugal the scare of their lives. Or unless it was the behaviour of those iron men from Argentina. 'Animals', Sir Alf Ramsey called them – a verdict that needed a decade before it was forgiven.

England's most significant stepping stone towards the world championship was negotiated six months before the finals – in December 1965 – when they beat the champions of Europe, Spain, in Madrid. It was not the fact but the manner of the victory that was important. Ramsey decided to pull back an extra attacker from the normal 4-2-4 system to tighten the midfield defence. Bobby Charlton was withdrawn from the wing to a midfield role, alongside his pugnacious little Manchester United colleague Nobby Stiles and the stylish George Eastham. 4-3-3 was born, the Spaniards were beaten 2-0 at a canter and England were ready to take on the world.

Even so, they could not break down the defensive screen of the boring Uruguayans in the first match of the 1966 tournament. Uruguay played with eight or nine men massed in defence. It was the epitome of modern World Cups – a goalless draw. Few of the partisan Wembley crowd could have thought afterwards that there was any way in which this England side could produce enough attacking flair to win the trophy. But they did.

Their next game, against Mexico, at least produced a Bobby Charlton 'special'. It needed his breathtaking shot to the top corner of the net from 30 yards to break what looked like being another deadlock. He was now England's midfield general. His brother Jack was the pivot of the back four. Skipper Bobby Moore, playing alongside him, was an inspiration with his tackling, his reading of the game and his distribution. Behind them, England undoubtedly had the finest goalkeeper in the world in Gordon Banks. Against Mexico, Ramsey introduced the West Ham player Martin Peters as a kind of false left winger in a number 11 shirt who could drift into goalscoring positions from midfield. In attack, the willing workhorse was Roger Hunt, and it was he who wrapped up the 2-0 win over Mexico with the second goal. Mexico's second choice goalkeeper was the amazing veteran Carbajal, making World Cup history by playing in his fifth successive Final series.

Meanwhile, on the Everton club ground in Liverpool, Brazil were starting what turned out to be their most disastrous World Cup of all. They began well enough, if not exactly inspirationally, against Bulgaria. In fact, Pelé's blistering

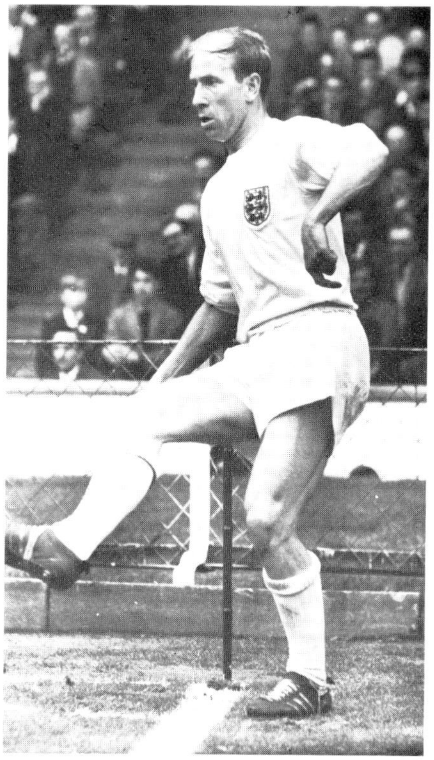

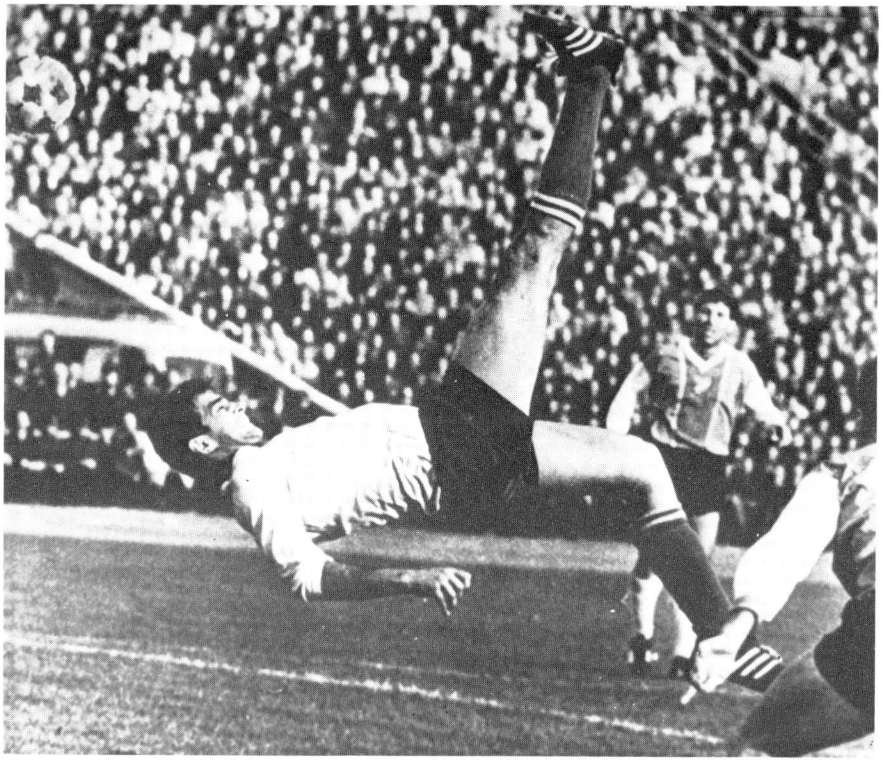

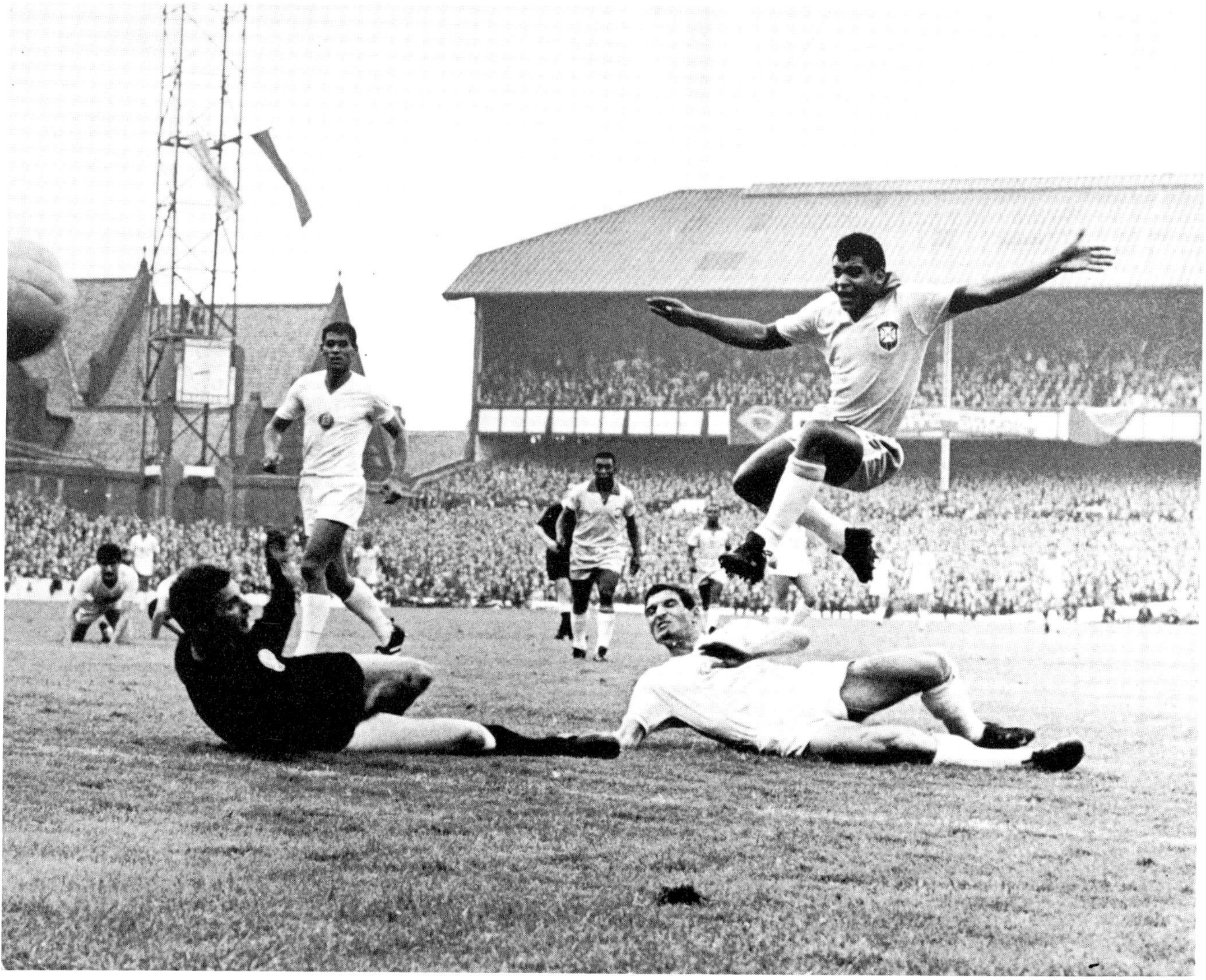

left **Two players who delighted British crowds in 1966 were Bene and Albert, Hungarians who were particularly brilliant in Hungary's win over Brazil.**

right **Eusebio shows his power with a blistering shot which scored against Bulgaria.**

free kick goal was the first of the tournament, but it was not an omen; far more so was Bulgaria's tackling.

Although Garrincha's famous 'banana' shot produced a second free kick goal for the holders, the 2-0 win was soured by Jetchev's treatment of Pelé. It seemed that he was never restrained by the English referee Jim Finney. Worse was to follow for Brazil – and Pelé. Their next opponents were Hungary. The countries had not met in the World Cup since the notorious 'Battle of Berne' in 1954, the last time Brazil had been beaten. Now Brazil were without Pelé, unfit after the first match injuries. Hungary had the superbly gifted Florian Albert playing a Hidegkuti deep-lying role; they had Matrai as sweeper and only two real strikers, the quicksilver Bene and the deadly Farkas. But when they broke, they pushed men forward with devastating speed. It was a miserable, wet night. It would be a black one for Brazil.

Within three minutes, Bene cut through from the wing to put Hungary ahead. The nineteen-

below **Goalkeeper Szentmihalyi saved this flying Brazilian header, but his mistakes later against Portugal proved costly.**

year-old Tostao, playing his first World Cup match, equalised when Lima's free kick rebounded to him. But Albert was now supreme and, after half-time, he and Bene combined to set up one of the great goals of the tournament for Farkas. The break on the right was, as ever, like lightning, and the finish was an unstoppable volley in full stride. The watching millions on television sensed the champions were down and nearly out, especially when Meszoly's penalty wrapped up a 3-1 win for Hungary. But it was Portugal who delivered Brazil's coup de grâce.

Brazil desperately made nine changes. Seven men played their first World Cup match against the Portuguese and their veteran goalkeeper Gilmar was replaced by the tall Manga. His nerves showed and his weak punch from a cross by Eusebio after only fourteen minutes allowed Simoes, Portugal's lively little winger, to head the first goal. Before half-time, the giant Torres at centre-forward for Portugal, headed on Coluna's free kick and the irrepressible Eusebio was on it in a flash to head home. The turning point for Brazil came in the second half with a dreadful foul on Pelé by Morais. With the socks rolled down and his face racked in pain, Brazil's greatest star limped out of the tournament. Rildo did manage to pull one goal back for the brave Brazilians but Eusebio finished them off with his second goal, from a corner. Brazil were out and Portugal, who had already beaten Hungary 3-1 thanks to a couple of errors by goalkeeper Szentmihalyi, went through with maximum points. Hungary joined them with a similar win over Bulgaria in their final match. Either of these qualifiers looked a far better bet at this stage to take the trophy than England.

The home side had laboured to beat France 2-0 in their final match. Both goals came from the willing Hunt but the win was soured by an injury to Herbin and blemished by a controversial foul by the aggressive Stiles on Simon. FA officials insisted Ramsey should drop Stiles; Ramsey said he would rather resign. The matter was dropped – not Stiles.

Meanwhile, West Germany had suggested how serious Helmut Schoen's challenge for the trophy might be. In their opening match, in Sheffield, they devastated the Swiss 5-0. It was a victory helped by the suspension of Swiss stars Kuhn and Leimgruber for breaking bounds. But nonetheless it gave warning of the emergence of a truly gifted midfield player in

**top left France made their last appearance in the finals in 1966, before winning their way to Argentina in 1978. The 1966 squad was, left to right, standing: De Bourgoing, Bonnel, Guerin (trainer), Chiarisoli (chairman), Artelesa, Bosquier, Budzinski, de Michele, Gondet, Couecou, Barafe, Aubour, Schuth, Hausser, Combin. Front: Pinnin, Herbet, Blanchet, Robuschi, Herbin, Djorknest, Carnus, Simon, Chorda, Muller.**

Franz Beckenbauer. His attacking skills brought him two goals, and two more fell to the aggressive, blond inside forward Helmut Haller.

Argentina began with a 2-1 win over the other team in the group, Spain. They gave the Spanish schemer Luis Suarez some crude treatment and got both their goals from their fine centre-forward Luis Artime from openings by Ermindo Onega. When the two giants of this group met, the Germans became absurdly cautious and withdrew Beckenbauer as deep as they decided to play him against Bobby Charlton in the Final. It was an altogether ill-tempered match with no goals but with Albrecht, the Argentinian sweeper, sent off. A remarkable goal by Germany's big left winger Emmerich in the final qualifying game, against

Spain, gave them a 2-1 win which saw them through to the quarter-finals.

Meanwhile, in the north-east, there was the 'fairytale' rise of the little North Koreans at the expense of the fancied Italians. The odd eyebrow had been raised when the North Koreans drew 1-1 with Chile. Italy, however, had already beaten Chile 2-0 and the fact that they went down 1-0 to the mighty Russians did not suggest they were in decline. But the English, never over-fond of the Italians, had taken to the North Koreans'

they arrived back at Genoa airport. The team of Oriental unknowns were no longer a bar-room joke. Their months of monastic seclusion and preparation had paid off. They were in the quarter-finals, along with the all-conquering Russians. And still they had not reached their zenith! It came in the quarter-final against Portugal at Everton.

After twenty-four minutes, an unbelieving world audience heard the score, North Korea 3 Portugal 0. Surely the little men were not going to take the whole tourna-

opposite right **The Mexican team warmed up in Switzerland on their way to the finals. Left to right: Diaz, Jara, Chaires, Hernandez, Padilla, Fragoso, Nurez, Cisneros, Ruvalcaba, Calderon, Pena.**

opposite below **Enrique Borja (20) congratulated by Mexican teammates after scoring the goal in the 1-1 draw with France.**

blend of non-stop aggression and total disrespect for reputations. The Middlesbrough crowd applauded when Bulgarelli had to limp off after trying to foul a Korean, and cheered when, in his absence, Pak Doo Ik, North Korea's inside left, scored the historic goal which gave them victory – a goal which cost the Italian manager Fabbri his job and his team a tomato bombardment when

ment by storm. But then Eusebio took over. He scored twice before half-time, once from the penalty spot. Two more in the second half, including a second penalty, gave him four and, with one more from Augusto, Portugal eventually went through 5-3. But the North Koreans would never be forgotten. What a way to go!

That glittering quarter-final was in vivid contrast to the mediocre

above **The happy North Korean team celebrate after one of the greatest World Cup surprises of all time – their 1-0 win over mighty Italy.**

affair at Sunderland which saw the end of the mercurial Hungarians at the hands of the Russians. Hungary had suffered bad goalkeeping all the way along and this time Gelei was responsible for both Russian goals, fumbling a shot and then failing to hold a cross. For Hungary, Bene scored one and Rakosi missed the simplest of chances. So Russia beat the technically superior Hungarians 2-1.

The other two quarter-finals were a disgrace in sporting terms. At Wembley, where England were to play all six matches, Argentina earned their 'animals' title from Sir Alf Ramsey. The Argentinian captain, the huge, arrogant Antonio Rattin, was eventually sent off just before half-time by Herr Kreitlein, the West German referee. But Rattin thought he was victimised and refused to leave the field. Eventually, on the brink of apparent disaster, after a delay of eight minutes, he went. And England eventually went through. Rattin and his team had been more concerned with obstructing England and trying to intimidate them than playing football. England could not break down a ruth-

Opposite above **Russia played Chile** in the 1966 finals (they refused to on political grounds in the 1978 qualifying competition) and won 2-1. The Russian goalkeeper punches clear.

opposite below **Bulgarian defender Davidov** deflects a shot by Bene past the despairing leap of their goalkeeper for Hungary's equalizer. Hungary won 3-1.

left above **Yashin** saves as Albert (Hungary) moves in and Voronin (Russia) keeps watch in the quarter final won 2-1 by Russia.

left centre **Rattin**, the Argentinian captain, was sent off by West German referee Kreitlin, but the match was held up for several minutes while he argued.

below **Geoff Hurst** heads in a cross by Martin Peters to score the only goal of the infamous England-Argentina quarter-final.

55

right **Uruguay's goalkeeper Mazurkiewicz was beaten four times in the quarter-final against West Germany. This is the third goal, scored by Seeler.**

below **The Portuguese team which played attractive football throughout the 1966 finals. Left to right, back: Baptista, Morais, Graca, Conceicao, Lucas, Pereira. Front: Augusto, Torres, Eusebio, Coluna, Simoes.**

opposite above **Nobby Stiles of England marked Eusebio of Portugal closely in the semi-final. Here Eusebio gets in a header despite Stiles' proximity.**

opposite below **Eusebio, the most gifted striker of the 1966 finals, left the field in tears after England beat Portugal 2-1 in one of the best matches of the whole tournament.**

56

less defence or beat Roma in goal until Hurst, replacing Greaves in the attack, angled home a beautiful header from a cross by his West Ham team-mate Martin Peters thirteen minutes from time.

At Hillsborough, Sheffield, the temperament of the Uruguayans underlined South America's bad name. After Schnellinger appeared to handle on the line with impunity and then Held's shot was freakishly deflected into the Uruguayan net by Haller, they could not contain themselves. Troche was sent off for kicking Emmerich and Silva for fouling Haller. The remaining nine men were overrun in the second half and Germany won 4-0.

The Everton semi-final between Germany and Russia was a squalid affair. The Russians had Sabo limping and Chislenko sent off for kicking Held, after himself being badly injured by Schnellinger. Haller and Beckenbauer got the goals but even against nine fit men, Germany struggled to hold

57

out and Porkujan actually pulled it back to 2-1 when goalkeeper Tilkowski faltered two minutes from time.

The other semi-final saw England at last emerge as something more than a disciplined outfit with home advantage. Their qualifying group 'flirtation' with wingers – Connelly, Paine and Callaghan – was over, Hurst was back in favour alongside Hunt in attack and Bobby Charlton linked from midfield with all his innate attacking genius. He destroyed Portugal, scoring both England's goals. The first was a follow-up after Pereira had only managed to parry Hunt's shot and the second a shot of bullet-like speed and accuracy from Hurst's pass. The other man-of-the-match for England was the gap-toothed Nobby Stiles who stuck to Eusebio like a leech. Even so, Eusebio scored his eighth World Cup goal eight minutes from time. It was a penalty conceded by Jack Charlton, and the first goal against England in the tournament. So tears for Eusebio and Portugal, even though they took third place 2-1 against the Russians with Eusebio scoring again from the penalty spot.

Now only West Germany stood between England and Alf Ramsey's prophecy. The drama of that brilliant English summer's day matched the setting – a packed Wembley and, outside, a world-wide audience of 400,000,000 television viewers.

The Germans saw Bobby Charlton as the danger man and withdrew Beckenbauer from his natural attacking role into a defensive shadowing job. Even so, they scored first. England fullback Wilson could only head out weakly in the fourteenth minute and Haller shot home; 1-0 to Germany. But within six minutes, the West Ham club 'telepathy' brought England level. Skipper Bobby Moore needed no more than a glance to see his clubmate Geoff Hurst poised to dart into a space in the German area. The free kick was inch-perfect and Hurst's header matched it; 1-1. The other West Ham player, Martin Peters, pounced to make it 2-1 with a vicious volley twelve minutes from time. The Cup was surely

opposite above **Bobby Moore** leading England in the 1966 Final.

opposite centre **Geoff Hurst**, England's three-goal hero, gets up above the West German defence to get in a header.

opposite below **Helmut Haller**, of West Germany, scorer of the first goal in the Final, leaves Alan Ball, one of England's stars, groping.

left above **West Germany's dramatic last-minute equalizer in the 1966 Final. Wolfgang Weber gets the ball home despite the lunging attempt to block by Ray Wilson and the dive of Gordon Banks. Other players Uwe Seeler, George Cohen (on ground), Bobby Moore (with upstretched arm), Karl-Heinz Schnellinger and Jack Charlton.**

left centre **Geoff Hurst (right) scores his second goal in extra time to give England the lead. The ball bounced down from the cross bar and the linesman decided it crossed the line.**

bottom **The scoreboard read 'England 3 Germany 2' as this rocket shot from Geoff Hurst registered his hat-trick and wrapped up the game 4-2 for England.**

59

**The progress of the Jules Rimet trophy after the 1966 Final.** Right **England skipper Bobby Moore receives it from the Queen, with Sir Stanley Rous and the Duke of Edinburgh watching.** Below **The Cup held in triumph by Moore as he is chaired by colleagues (from the left) Jack Charlton, Stiles, Banks, Ball, Peters, Hurst, Wilson, Cohen and Bobby Charlton.** Below right **The Cup shown to England manager Alf Ramsey as he congratulates Stiles.**

England's now. But, in the very last minute, Jack Charlton was judged to have fouled Held, when the free kick might well have gone the other way. Emmerich's drive rebounded to Weber, who squeezed home an equaliser at the far post. Extra-time.

'You've won it once. Now go out and win it again', Ramsey told his stricken and deflated team. The relentless running of the red-haired Alan Ball was an inspiration and example to his elders. He would never give up. Eventually, he laid back a beautiful pass for Hurst, the shot cannoned down off the crossbar, and Hunt, poised for the final touch, turned away with his arms raised. Goal–or was it? The Germans thought the ball had not crossed the line, the Russian linesman disagreed. England back in front. And, as if to answer the doubters, Hurst took a pass from his captain Moore, galloped into the German penalty area and rifled home a superb left-foot shot for the first World Cup Final hat-trick. Now it *was* all over.

Players, officials and reserves all leaped in ecstasy. They shrieked in relief as much as delight. Some knelt, most cried. But Alf Ramsey –the architect of victory–was apparently unmoved. He simply sat, for a moment, sharing the joy of his players. None of them could quite share *his* satisfaction. Just as he had lifted Ipswich Town from the Third to the First Division championship without a superabundance of talent, this had been a triumph for organisation and a system of play which blended players and gave them a unique understanding. The supremely gifted Jimmy Greaves had to sit and watch the final triumph of a team bred on collective perspiration rather than individual inspiration. 'Work rate' they called it. And it may have contributed more than anything to England's dwindling supply of truly World class players in succeeding World Cups.

The BBC's 1966 television Sportsview Personality of the Year and the International Personality were both World Cup figures, Bobby Moore, the winning skipper, who brought along the Cup itself to the presentation, and Eusebio, the leading goalscorer.

## 8th WORLD CUP England, 1966

### GROUP 1
England (0)0 Uruguay (0)0
France (0)1 Mexico (0)1
Hausser — Borja
Uruguay (2)2 France (1)1
Rocha, Cortes — De Bourgoing (pen)
England (1)2 Mexico (0)0
Charlton, Hunt
Uruguay (0)0 Mexico (0)0
England (1)2 France (0)0
Hunt 2

|  | P | W | D | L | F | A | Pts |
|---|---|---|---|---|---|---|---|
| England | 3 | 2 | 1 | 0 | 4 | 0 | 5 |
| Uruguay | 3 | 1 | 2 | 0 | 2 | 1 | 4 |
| Mexico | 3 | 0 | 2 | 1 | 1 | 3 | 2 |
| France | 3 | 0 | 1 | 2 | 2 | 5 | 1 |

### GROUP 2
West Germany (3)5 Switzerland (0)0
Held, Haller 2 (1 pen), Beckenbauer 2
Argentina (0)2 Spain (0)1
Artime 2 — Pirri
Spain (0)2 Switzerland (1)1
Sanchis, Amancio — Quentin
Argentina (0)0 W. Germany (0)0
Argentina (0)2 Switzerland (0)0
Artime, Onega
West Germany (1)2 Spain (1)1
Emmerich, Seeler — Fuste

|  | P | W | D | L | F | A | Pts |
|---|---|---|---|---|---|---|---|
| West Germany | 3 | 2 | 1 | 0 | 7 | 1 | 5 |
| Argentina | 3 | 2 | 1 | 0 | 4 | 1 | 5 |
| Spain | 3 | 1 | 0 | 2 | 4 | 5 | 2 |
| Switzerland | 3 | 0 | 0 | 3 | 1 | 9 | 0 |

### GROUP 3
Brazil (1)2 Bulgaria (0)0
Pele, Garrincha
Portugal (1)3 Hungary (0)1
Augusto 2, Torres — Bene
Hungary (1)3 Brazil (1)1
Bene, Farkas, Meszoly (pen) — Tostao
Portugal (2)3 Bulgaria (0)0
Vutzov (og), Eusebio, Torres
Portugal (2)3 Brazil (0)1
Simoes, Eusebio 2 — Rildo
Hungary (2)3 Bulgaria (1)1
Davidov (og), Meszoly, Bene — Asparoukhov

|  | P | W | D | L | F | A | Pts |
|---|---|---|---|---|---|---|---|
| Portugal | 3 | 3 | 0 | 0 | 9 | 2 | 6 |
| Hungary | 3 | 2 | 0 | 1 | 7 | 5 | 4 |
| Brazil | 3 | 1 | 0 | 2 | 4 | 6 | 2 |
| Bulgaria | 3 | 0 | 0 | 3 | 1 | 8 | 0 |

### GROUP 4
USSR (2)3 North Korea (0)0
Malafeev 2, Banischevski
Italy (1)2 Chile (0)0
Mazzola, Barison
Chile (1)1 North Korea (0)1
Marcos (pen) — Pak Seung Jin
USSR (0)1 Italy (0)0
Chislenko
North Korea (1)1 Italy (0)0
Pak Doo Ik
USSR (1)2 Chile (1)1
Porkujan 2 — Marcos

|  | P | W | D | L | F | A | Pts |
|---|---|---|---|---|---|---|---|
| USSR | 3 | 3 | 0 | 0 | 6 | 1 | 6 |
| North Korea | 3 | 1 | 1 | 1 | 2 | 4 | 3 |
| Italy | 3 | 1 | 0 | 2 | 2 | 2 | 2 |
| Chile | 3 | 0 | 1 | 2 | 2 | 5 | 1 |

### QUARTER-FINALS
England (0)1 Argentina (0)0
Hurst
West Germany (1)4 Uruguay (0)0
Held, Beckenbauer, Seeler, Haller
Portugal (2)5 North Korea (3)3
Eusebio 4 (2 pens), Augusto — Pak Seung Jin, Yang Sung Kook, Li Dong Woon
USSR (1)2 Hungary (0)1
Chislenko, Porkujan — Bene

### SEMI-FINALS
West Germany (1)2 USSR (0)1
Haller, Beckenbauer — Porkujan
England (1)2 Portugal (0)1
Charlton (R) 2 — Eusebio (pen)

### THIRD PLACE MATCH: Wembley
Portugal (1)2 USSR (1)1
Eusebio (pen), Torres — Malafeev

### FINAL: Wembley 30.7.66
Attendance 93,000
England (1)(2)4 West Germany (1)(2)2
Hurst 3, Peters — Haller, Weber
**England:** Banks; Cohen, Wilson; Stiles, Charlton (J), Moore (capt); Ball, Hurst, Hunt, Charlton (R), Peters
**West Germany:** Tilkowski; Hottges, Schnellinger; Beckenbauer, Schulz, Weber; Held, Haller, Seeler (capt), Overath, Emmerich
**Referee:** Dienst (Switzerland)

### LEADING SCORERS
9—Eusebio (Portugal) (4 pens)
5—Haller (West Germany) (1 pen)
4—Beckenbauer (West Germany)
Hurst (England)
Porkujan (USSR)

# 1970 MEXICO

FIFA membership: 138

Entries: 73

Finals: Four qualifying groups; quarter-finals onwards, knock-out

Grounds: Mexico City, Puebla, Toluca, Guadalajara, Leon

Leading scorer: Müller (West Germany) 10 goals

Winners: Brazil

---

The 1970 World Cup finals threw up all sorts of question marks. Could England, with the backbone of their 1966 winning side still available, prove themselves as good a team away from home or would the real European challenge come rather from West Germany or European Champions Italy? Could Pelé, Tostao and Jairzinho inspire a new generation of Brazilians to complete a unique third victory? Or would the much-vaunted Peru team managed by the Brazilian Didi pick up where Brazil had left off in Chile? They had after all put out Argentina en route for Mexico. But the biggest question remained... how would European teams cope with the problems of altitude and extreme heat? To make matters worse, the games would be played in the noon-day sun to satisfy the schedules of European TV stations.

Certainly Sir Alf Ramsey was not venturing any predictions this time. For their part, the Brazilians had scarcely had an ideal build-up. Tostao had suffered a serious eye injury, the team had lost form and their manager, a volatile ex-journalist and former boss of the club side Botafogo, Joao Saldanha, had unwisely fallen out with Pelé. The trial of strength could only go one way. On the eve of the finals, Saldanha was replaced by Mario Zagalo, left winger in the winning sides of 1958 and 1962. Tostao made a surprising recovery and morale was restored. But Brazil remained suspect in goal and defence generally.

Italy relied heavily on the Cagliari striker Luigi Riva. Germany had Beckenbauer and Overath from 1966 and had now unearthed a stocky goal-scoring 'machine' called Gerd Müller. Manager Schoen had also recalled the veteran Seeler, with three World Cups already behind him.

The 'explosion' of Black Power in FIFA had earned Africa its first representative in the finals, though Morocco, under a Yugoslav coach, found the going tough. Also facing their first finals were Israel, winners of the Asia and Oceania group, and, from the Central American group, El

opposite above **An emblem seller in Puebla before the World Cup 1970. He is holding a pennant for Sweden, and pennants and badges are on display for all the countries.**

opposite below **Part of the opening ceremony in the Aztec Stadium, Mexico City.**

left above **The Russians of 1970. Left to right, front row: Zykov, Muntian, Puzach, Parkuian, Evriuzhikhin, Kiselev, Nodia, Serebriannikov, Khurtsilava, Metreveli, Lovchev, Back: Byshovets, Kavazashvili, Logofet, Asatiana, Paramonov (coach), Kachalin (senior coach), Kaplichni, Dzodzvashvili, Papaer, Shesternev, Afonin, Khmelnitski, Rudakov.**

far left **Kaplichni of Russia stretches to beat Fragoso of Mexico in the opening game.**

left **Scorer in every round of the tournament, Brazil's great winger Jairzinho.**

Salvador. The latter's qualification at the expense of her bitter rival and neighbour Honduras sparked off the so-called 'Football War' which cost an estimated 3,000 lives. So, a diffuse line-up but there was no doubt at all about which country started as villains.

England were far better prepared than in 1966. A South American tour the year before had yielded a goalless draw in Mexico, an excellent 2-1 win in Uruguay and a narrow 2-1 defeat in Brazil. Banks, Moore and Bobby Charlton, Ramsey's three World class players were still there, together with the busy Ball, Jack Charlton, now second choice to Labone, Peters (labelled 'ten years ahead of his time' by Ramsey) and the combative Stiles, really brought along for morale since his job was now in the hands of Mullery. Ramsey had new attacking full-backs in Newton and Cooper and a stocky, aggressive centre-forward in Francis Lee. It was a 4-4-2 line-up. It was efficient, and when it left for the pre-Mexico warm-up games in Columbia and Ecuador it carried high hopes. But by the time England faced her first match of the 1970 finals in Guadalajara against Rumania, her image was rock bottom. Skipper Bobby Moore had been arrested in Bogota and 'framed' for the theft of a diamond bracelet. It was a ludicrous charge which eventually took years to clear up, though the England captain was freed in time to join his team for the first match. By then, Sir Alf Ramsey's totally businesslike lack of accommodation for the Mexican journalists who ignored his schedules doubled England's reputation as a bunch of villains. The feeling was pretty mutual after the booing of the Union Jack at the opening ceremony and the deliberate campaign of noise and disturbance outside the England hotel to prevent the players sleeping properly.

When Europe eventually got to grips with South America on the pitch it was clearly going to call for refereeing of the most diplomatic, not to say, firm kind. The opening game between Mexico and Russia, suffered from quite the wrong approach. Referee Tschensher from East Germany stuck to the book, penalised everything, and turned a tedious 0-0 draw into an endurance test for spectators. In contrast, England

top left **Pelé in action in Brazil's first match with Czechoslovakia.**

top right **Clodoaldo of Brazil shields the ball from England's Terry Cooper.**

above **Banks' great save from Pelé, one of the most famous saves in World Cup history. Tostao and Mullery watch.**

suffered some terrible excesses from the brutal Rumanians in her opening game under the eyes of an indulgent Belgian referee. Mocanu, the Rumanian left-back, lamed at least two England players but England deservedly won with a crisply-struck goal from Hurst.

Brazil, with Pelé and Jairzinho in superb form, recovered from the shock of falling behind to the Czechs in their first game. The television millions will long remember the shot of Petras falling to his knees, overcome with the emotion of that exhilarating shot. But the Brazilians could not be kept at bay and two misses by the Czechs proved costly. Rivelino scored with a searing free kick,

Pelé caught a Gerson pass on his chest, swivelled and scored another, and Jairzinho struck twice more. 4-1 flattered Brazil but it certainly set up the meeting between Brazil and England which many thought could be a rehearsal of the Final.

England were not helped by the disturbances around their hotel overnight, with throngs of Mexicans, unharassed by the police, chanting and hooting car horns until the small hours. Equipped with their 'slow sodium' pills, the England players went out to face the most talented side in the tournament in near 100-degree temperatures. At half-time it was goalless, thanks to one of the

top **Jairzinho shoots after being fed by Pelé (centre) and Brazil score the only goal of the match against England.**

above **England's nearest in the match with Brazil. Alan Ball's shot beats Felix but the ball hits the bar.**

65

greatest saves in World Cup history from Banks. Jairzinho's cross was met fair and square by Pelé with a header purposely bounced to beat the goalkeeper's dive, but somehow Banks, in a blur of reflexes, twisted backwards and up to scoop the ball over the bar. Even the astounded Pelé applauded. England had missed two great chances before Tostao held off three English defenders—literally in the case of the immaculate Moore—crossed from the left, Pelé rolled the ball on and Jairzinho thundered in to score. England's chance of a draw was tossed away by Ball and then, flagrantly, by Astle, one shot going too high, the other just wide of an open goal. Still, thanks to a slightly dubious penalty coolly converted by Clarke, which gave them their victory over the Czechs, England accompanied Brazil into the quarter-finals.

Meanwhile, there was every sign that Italy were terrified of another North Korean trauma. They were disrupted by a major row over the dropping of Gianni Rivera in favour of Sandro Mazzola. In the end it needed Italian Federation President, Artemo Franchi, to intervene. Team manager Ferruccio Valcareggi compromised by using both players, Mazzola in the first half, Rivera in the second. This was possible because the 1970 finals saw the introduction of substitutes. Managers now had to think in terms of squads of thirteen players and England's Ramsey, for one, did not find that easy.

Italy scraped through their opening game 1-0 against Sweden thanks to a goalkeeping error. Then they drew goallessly against both Uruguay and little Israel, who had already forced a 1-1 draw with Sweden. So, typically it seemed, Italy with one solitary goal and two draws made the quarter-finals, along with Uruguay, who pipped Sweden on goal average despite losing 1-0 to them in their final match.

In Group 1, in Mexico City, the host country only dropped that opening point to Russia (who qualified with them) but they were fortunate in both their other games. Against El Salvador, one of their four goals came from a free

opposite **The world's best attacker and the world's best defender. Pelé of Brazil and Moore of England congratulate each other after the Brazil-England match.**

top left **Albertosi, the Italian goalkeeper, catches the ball in Italy's 0-0 draw with Uruguay.**

top right **Another Italian 0-0 draw. Sandro Mazzola, who alternated with Rivera in Italy's midfield, beats a tackle against Israel.**

above **Franz Beckenbauer fails to rob Colin Bell in the West Germany-England quarter-final.**

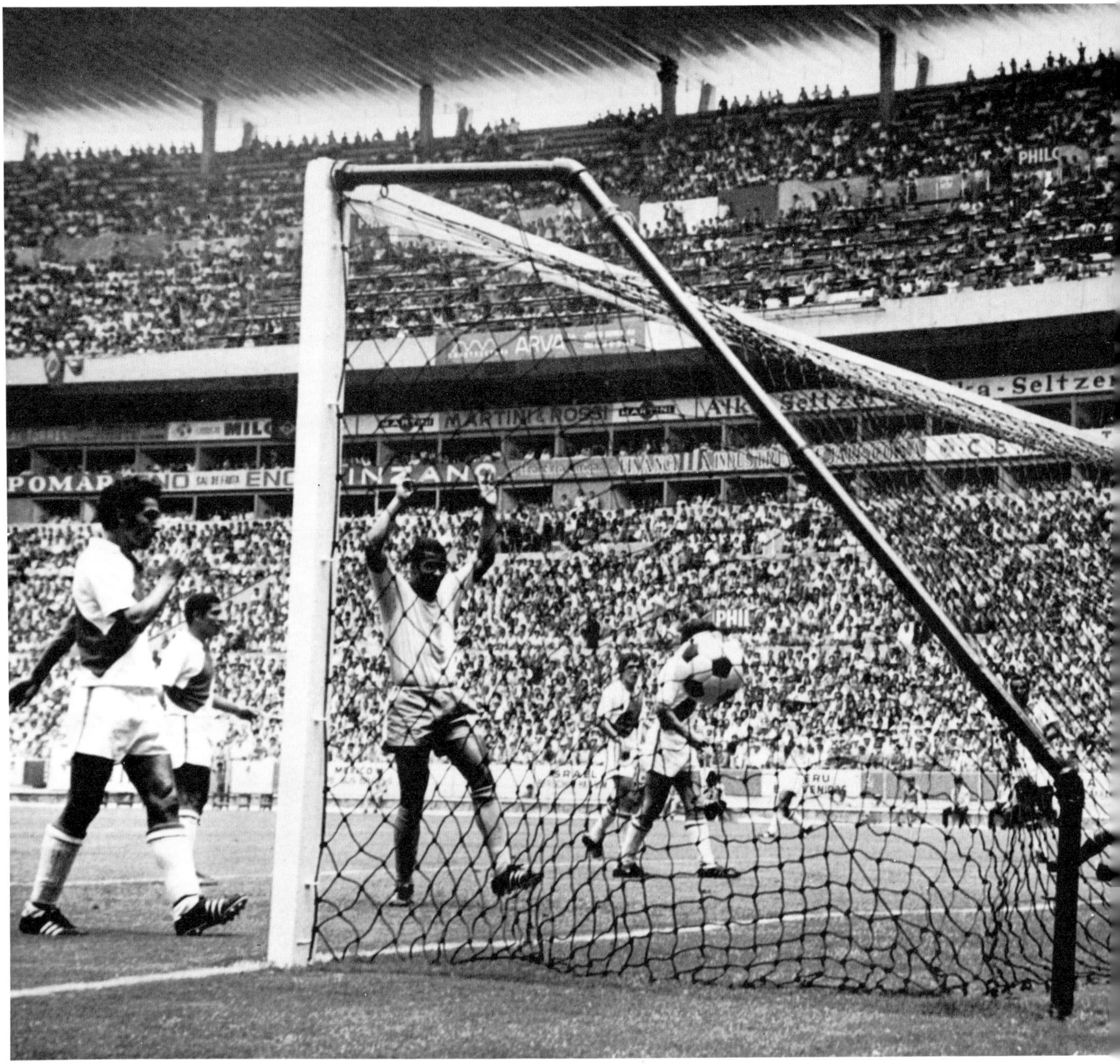
ARVA
MARTINI & ROSSI
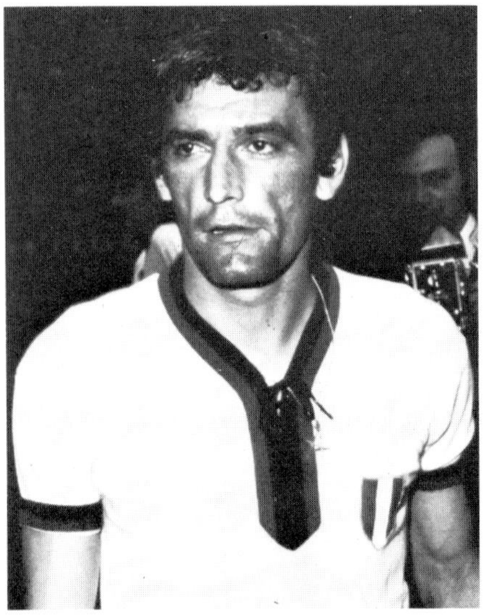
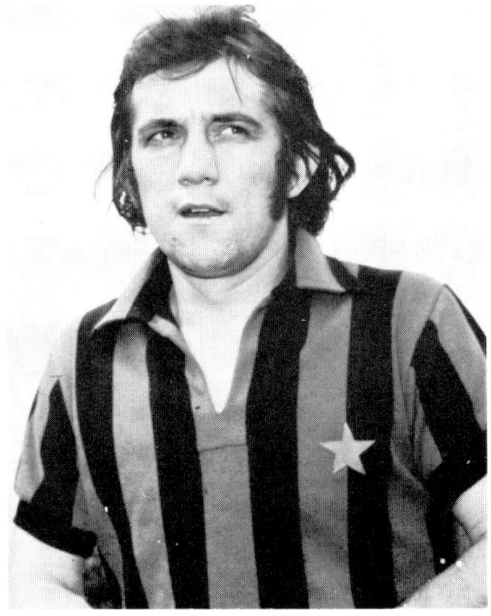
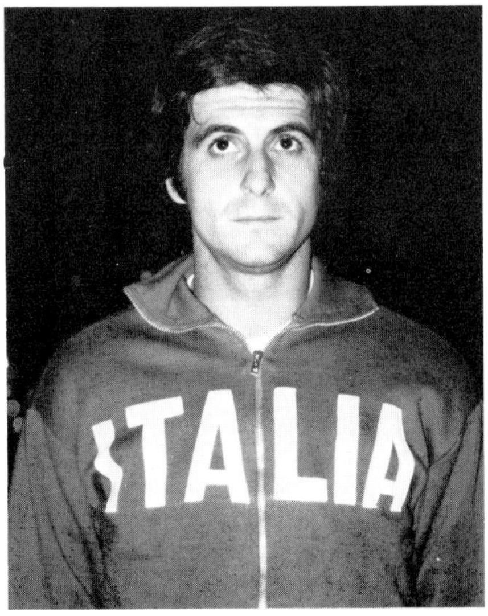
ITALIA

left **The quarter-final between Brazil and Peru. Tostao (behind referee) beats Rubinos, the Peru goalkeeper, from a narrow angle to score in Brazil's 4-2 victory.**

below **Giacinto Facchetti, one of Italy's defensive stalwarts.**

Bottom, left to right **Five players from the see-saw semi-final between Italy and West Germany: Luigi Riva, Italy's main striker, who scored; Roberto Boninsegna, Italy's winger whose early goal divided the sides for over 80 minutes; Gianni Rivera, who scored the extra-time winner which gave Italy a 4-3 win; German captain Franz Beckenbauer, who played with his shoulder strapped; Gerd Muller, the tournament's top scorer, who scored two of West Germany's goals.**

kick awarded to the opposition but taken by Mexico! The only goal of their game against Belgium came from a very doubtful penalty. The Belgians were their own worst enemies, falling out between themselves over the use of boots from the rival firms Adidas and Puma. A similar row in the Czech camp, in Guadalajara, led to the team being suspended. Belgium had an outstanding goalkeeper in Christian Piot but their only success was against El Salvador, who returned home without a goal or a point to their credit.

In Group 4, in Leon, West Germany had a terrible shock against Morocco. They trailed to a goal from Houmane until late in the game when goals from Seeler and Müller saved their faces. But the revelation of this group were Peru. Chumpitaz drove them from the back and their superbly built winger Cubillas was always an explosive threat. Peru, who had come from a country stricken by earthquakes, had to recover from being two goals down to Bulgaria before winning 3-2 in the opening game, and they then disposed of Morocco 3-0 with two more goals for Cubillas. But, after the fright provided by the Moroccans, the Germans found their stride and Müller emphasised his deadly touch with hat-tricks in both the 5-2 win over Bulgaria and the 3-1 victory against Peru, who still went through.

In the quarter-final, West Germany had ground advantage over England. Leon was their base, and it was at higher altitude than England's previous base at Guadalajara. Worse still for England, their goalkeeper Banks was taken ill and missed the game. His deputy, Peter Bonetti, had not played for a month, and was blamed for at least one, if not all three, of the German goals. Yet England got off to a magnificent start. Mullery made and scored the first goal; Peters added a second in the second half and they looked home and dry. But, surprisingly, Ramsey substituted both Peters and Bobby Charlton – his last international appearance – while the Germans brought on their trump card in the shape of winger Grabowski. It was 2-1 when Beckenbauer's shot bounced under Bonetti's body, and then a remarkable back-header by Seeler brought the scores level and sent the game into extra-time. Finally, the comeback was complete as Müller volleyed the winner for West Germany.

In Guadalajara, Brazil halted Peru 4-2 with two goals from Tostao and one each from Rivelino and Jairzinho. Felix in goal for Brazil was never at ease and Cubillas struck again for Peru. In Mexico City, there were bitter arguments about Uruguay's winning goal in extra-time against Russia. It seemed certain the ball had gone out of play before Cubilla crossed for Esparrago to score the only goal of the game. At Toluca, Italy at last lived up to their potential by thrashing Mexico 4-1. Riva scored two and Rivera, who galvanised the Italian attack when he came on at 1-1 at half-time, got another.

Now the Italians faced West Germany in Mexico City in the semi-final. The Germans, exhausted from their extra-time duel with England, were a goal down at half-time but sent the match into extra-time with a goal in injury time from Schnellinger. Then their hopes vanished with the shoulder injury to the brilliant Beckenbauer. Müller scored two more but the Italians, at last drawn out of their defensive shell, finally got the winner through Rivera.

In Guadalajara, Uruguay exposed Felix's frailty early on. Cubilla's narrow, angled shot literally bounced past him. It was only late in the first half that Clodoaldo, growing in stature with every game, burst through on the blind side to equalise. Felix had to make one magnificent save from Cubilla's header but with fourteen minutes left, Jairzinho climaxed a great run with Brazil's second, and in the last minute Rivelino made absolutely sure.

Italy's defensive approach to the Final rebounded on them badly. For Pelé it was a finale. He was in glorious form and put Brazil in front with a header from Rivelino's cross in eighteen minutes. A silly back-heel by Clodoaldo seven minutes before half-time allowed Boninsegna to put Italy level. But thereafter, Gerson was given the

opposite A sequence showing the winning goal in the Italy-West Germany semi-final. (1) Rivera (not in the picture) shoots and West Germany's goalkeeper Sepp Maier lunges at the ball. (2) The ball beats him. (3) The Italians show jubilation. (4) Maier expresses his frustration as Beckenbauer, with his right arm strapped, goes to retrieve the ball and seek yet another equalizer.

above The first goal in the Final. Pelé turns to greet his team-mates after his header had found the corner of the Italian net.

right Rivelino of Brazil beats Italy's Bertini but is brought down by the follow-through.

freedom of the midfield for Brazil and his fine left-foot shot from outside the box after sixty-six minutes swung the game Brazil's way. The third came when Pelé touched Gerson's free kick to the onrushing Jairzinho and finally, skipper Carlos Alberto, who had found so much space down the right flank, closed in to score an exciting fourth goal. Jairzinho had scored in every round; Pelé had escaped the 'hatchet men' to climax his World Cup career with a third win. Brazil were to keep the Jules Rimet trophy. South American football at its best was on top of the world again, and Brazilians at home celebrated.

opposite top **Rosato, Facchetti and Domenghini** of Italy line up to try to stop Brazil's Jairzinho.

opposite below **Carlos Alberto,** captain of Brazil, holds the World Cup aloft.

Zagalo, Brazil's manager, and Carlos Alberto, captain, show the Cup to crowds in Brasilia from a fire brigade truck during the team's rapturous welcome home.

## 9th WORLD CUP Mexico, 1970

### GROUP 1

| | | | |
|---|---|---|---|
| **Mexico** | (0)0 | USSR | (0)0 |
| **Belgium** | (1)3 | El Salvador | (0)0 |
| Van Moer 2, Lambert (pen) | | | |
| **USSR** | (1)4 | Belgium | (0)1 |
| Byshovets 2, Asatiani, | | Lambert | |
| Khmelnitsky | | | |
| **Mexico** | (1)4 | El Salvador | (0)0 |
| Valdivia 2, Fragoso, | | | |
| Bassguren | | | |
| **USSR** | (0)2 | El Salvador | (0)0 |
| Byshovets 2 | | | |
| **Mexico** | (1)1 | Belgium | (0)0 |
| Pena (pen) | | | |

| | P | W | D | L | F | A | Pts |
|---|---|---|---|---|---|---|---|
| USSR | 3 | 2 | 1 | 0 | 6 | 1 | 5 |
| Mexico | 3 | 2 | 1 | 0 | 5 | 0 | 5 |
| Belgium | 3 | 1 | 0 | 2 | 4 | 5 | 2 |
| El Savador | 3 | 0 | 0 | 3 | 0 | 9 | 0 |

### GROUP 2

| | | | |
|---|---|---|---|
| **Uruguay** | (1)2 | Israel | (0)0 |
| Maneiro, Mujica | | | |
| **Italy** | (1)1 | Sweden | (0)0 |
| Domenghini | | | |
| **Uruguay** | (0)0 | Italy | (0)0 |
| **Sweden** | (0)1 | Israel | (0)1 |
| Turesson | | Spiegler | |
| **Sweden** | (0)1 | Uruguay | (0)0 |
| Grahn | | | |
| **Italy** | (0)0 | Israel | (0)0 |

| | P | W | D | L | F | A | Pts |
|---|---|---|---|---|---|---|---|
| Italy | 3 | 1 | 2 | 0 | 1 | 0 | 4 |
| Uruguay | 3 | 1 | 1 | 1 | 2 | 1 | 3 |
| Sweden | 3 | 1 | 1 | 1 | 2 | 2 | 3 |
| Israel | 3 | 0 | 2 | 1 | 1 | 3 | 2 |

### GROUP 3

| | | | |
|---|---|---|---|
| **England** | (0)1 | Romania | (0)0 |
| Hurst | | | |
| **Brazil** | (1)4 | Czech. | (1)1 |
| Rivelino, Pele, | | Petras | |
| Jairzinho 2 | | | |
| **Romania** | (0)2 | Czech. | (1)1 |
| Neagu, Dumitrache | | Petras | |
| (pen) | | | |
| **Brazil** | (0)1 | England | (0)0 |
| Jairzinho | | | |
| **Brazil** | (2)3 | Romania | (0)2 |
| Pele 2, Jairzinho | | Dumitrache, | |
| | | Dembrovski | |
| **England** | (0)1 | Czech. | (0)0 |
| Clarke (pen) | | | |

| | P | W | D | L | F | A | Pts |
|---|---|---|---|---|---|---|---|
| Brazil | 3 | 3 | 0 | 0 | 8 | 3 | 6 |
| England | 3 | 2 | 0 | 1 | 2 | 1 | 4 |
| Romania | 3 | 1 | 0 | 2 | 4 | 5 | 2 |
| Czechoslovakia | 3 | 0 | 0 | 3 | 2 | 7 | 0 |

### GROUP 4

| | | | |
|---|---|---|---|
| **Peru** | (0)3 | Bulgaria | (1)2 |
| Gallardo, Chumpitaz, | | Dermendjiev, | |
| Cubillas | | Bonev | |
| **West Germany** | (0)2 | Morocco | (1)1 |
| Seeler, Muller | | Houmane | |
| **Peru** | (0)3 | Morocco | (0)0 |
| Cubillas 2, Challe | | | |
| **West Germany** | (2)5 | Bulgaria | (1)2 |
| Libuda, Muller 3 (1 pen), | | Nikodimov, Kolev | |
| Seeler | | | |
| **West Germany** | (3)3 | Peru | (1)1 |
| Muller 3 | | Cubillas | |
| **Bulgaria** | (1)1 | Morocco | (0)1 |
| Jetchev | | Ghazouani | |

| | P | W | D | L | F | A | Pts |
|---|---|---|---|---|---|---|---|
| West Germany | 3 | 3 | 0 | 0 | 10 | 4 | 6 |
| Peru | 3 | 2 | 0 | 1 | 7 | 5 | 4 |
| Bulgaria | 3 | 0 | 1 | 2 | 5 | 9 | 1 |
| Morocco | 3 | 0 | 1 | 2 | 2 | 6 | 1 |

### QUARTER-FINALS

| | | | |
|---|---|---|---|
| **Uruguay** | (0)(0)1 | USSR | (0)(0)0 |
| Esparrago | | | |
| **Italy** | (1)4 | Mexico | (1)1 |
| Domenghini, Riva 2, | | Gonzales | |
| Rivera | | | |
| **Brazil** | (2)4 | Peru | (1)2 |
| Rivelino, Tostao 2, | | Gallardo, Cubillas | |
| Jairzinho | | | |
| **West Germany** | (0)(2)3 | England | (1)(2)2 |
| Beckenbauer, Seeler, | | Mullery, Peters | |
| Muller | | | |

### SEMI-FINALS

| | | | |
|---|---|---|---|
| **Italy** | (1)(1)4 | W. Germany | (0)(1)3 |
| Boninsegna, Burgnich, | | Schnellinger, | |
| Riva, Rivera | | Muller 2 | |
| **Brazil** | (1)3 | Uruguay | (1)1 |
| Clodoaldo, Jairzinho, | | Cubilla | |
| Rivelino | | | |

**THIRD PLACE MATCH**: Mexico City 20.6.70
Attendance 80,000

| | | | |
|---|---|---|---|
| **West Germany** | (1)1 | Uruguay | (0)0 |
| Overath | | | |

**FINAL**: Mexico City 21.6.70
Attendance 110,000

| | | | |
|---|---|---|---|
| **Brazil** | (1)4 | Italy | (1)1 |
| Pele, Gerson, | | Boninsegna | |
| Jairzinho, Carlos Alberto | | | |

**Brazil**: Felix; Carlos Alberto, Brito, Wilson Piazza, Everaldo; Clodoaldo, Gerson; Jairzinho, Tostao, Pele, Rivelino

**Italy**: Albertosi; Burgnich, Cera, Rosato, Facchetti; Bertini, [Juliano], Mazzola, De Sisti; Domenghini, Boninsegna, [Rivera], Riva

**Referee**: Glockner (East Germany)

### LEADING SCORERS
10—Muller (West Germany)
7—Jairzinho (Brazil)
5—Cubillas (Peru)
4—Pele (Brazil), Byshovets (USSR)

73

# 1974 WEST GERMANY

FIFA membership: 140

Entries: 97

Finals: Four qualifying groups, two further pools to determine finalists and third/fourth places

Grounds: Dusseldorf, Munich, Stuttgart

Leading scorer: Lato (Poland) 7 goals

Winners: West Germany

---

So, a new World Cup, trophy and finals organised – and eventually won – with typical Germanic efficiency by the host country. Not only were they European champions, having beaten Russia 3-0 in 1972, but their side was built on a nucleus of six or more Bayern Munich players. Bayern, led by the masterly Beckenbauer with Müller as the prime marksman, had carried off the European Cup with a superb 4-0 replay victory over Atletico Madrid just a month before the World Cup finals. Both nationally and at club level Germany were on top in Europe. And remember the Final would be played in Munich, on Bayern's magnificent Olympic Stadium pitch. The South American threat had diminished. The biggest challenge would undoubtedly come from Holland. That tiny nation of some 13 million inhabitants had produced a generation of players of outstanding individual talent. Their captain Johan Cruyff was a player of explosive skills and artistic touch to compare with the great Pelé. Their manager was a tough Dutchman, Rinus Michels, who had successfully coached the great Ajax side during their three consecutive European Cup triumphs between 1971 and 1973. He was now in charge of the Spanish side Barcelona.

But, while Holland and Michels had reached Germany on a vastly better goal difference (not average this time) than neighbours Belgium, England – and Sir Alf Ramsey – had gone. They had dropped a fatal home point to Wales and left themselves needing to beat Poland at Wembley to qualify. On a night of astonishing escapes that would have made Houdini jealous, Poland and their awkward-looking goalkeeper

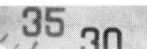

Tomaszewski survived for a 1-1 draw. For the first time since their entry in 1950, England had not made the finals, and three months later Ramsey was sacked, to be replaced eventually by Leeds United's Don Revie.

It made it no easier for an Englishman to accept his disappointment that Scotland had put out Czechoslovakia to qualify. Scotland, a team newly managed by Willie Ormond and skippered by the red-headed Leeds firebrand Billy Bremner, was right up to the finals rent with disputes over commercial ventures and apparent ill-discipline among the players. It was hardly the ideal preparation to face a qualifying group containing Brazil and Yugoslavia, even though Brazil were now bereft of Gerson, Tostao, Clodoaldo and Pelé. Yugoslavia, a menacing blend of physical strength and impressive skill, had qualified by beating Spain 1-0 in a play-off.

Russia did not compete because, having won a qualifying group containing the Republic of Ireland and France, they were required to play-off against the winners of South American Group 3, which happened to be Chile. The Soviets refused to play the away leg in Chile in the stadium where, they said, political prisoners had been imprisoned and tortured, so FIFA had no option but to give Chile a walk-over.

There were two largely unknown quantities this time. The 'Socceroos' from Australia had emerged from the Asia and Oceania Group for their first ever finals under the same Yugoslav coach, Rale Rasic, who had guided Morocco to the 1970 finals. And Haiti had put out Mexico in qualifying from Central America.

The one curiosity of the draw for the finals was the pairing in the same group of the hosts, West Germany, and their Communist brothers from across the Iron Curtain, East Germany. With memories of the tragedy of the Munich Olympics of 1972, when Israeli competitors were kidnapped and shot, those responsible for security heaved a sigh. They need not have done. The only security at risk was the West German team's defence. It would be their only defeat of the tournament.

opposite **The World Cup emblem formed by 2,000 schoolchildren on the field before the opening match between Brazil and Yugolavia.**

top **The Australian squad for 1974, taking part in their first World Cup finals.**

above **The team manager of Holland, the most attractive team in the tournament, Rinus Michels.**

75

The arrangements for the finals harked right back to 1950. From each of the initial four qualifying groups, two teams would go through to two further groups – in Brazil in 1950 only the preliminary group winners went forward. The winners of these two further groups would meet in the Final and the runners-up would dispute third and fourth places.

West Germany made heavy weather of their preliminary games. There was unrest in their training camp near Hamburg. They complained of the discipline. They also missed the midfield inspiration of the blond-haired Gunter Netzer, who was injured and out of form after a bad session in Spain with Real Madrid. With the eyes of the world and a packed Olympic Stadium in Berlin on them, Helmut Schoen's team only scraped home 1-0 against Chile, thanks to a crackerjack shot from their shock-headed defender Paul Breitner, Netzer's team-mate in Spain. The East Germans were meanwhile not finding Australia exactly a push-over in Hamburg. It took them until the fifty-ninth minute to find a way through and even then it was with an own goal as Sparwasser's shot was turned into his own net by Curran. The spell had been broken and twelve minutes later Streich hooked Vogel's centre in for a glorious second goal.

Against the West Germans, Australia might well have scored twice in the second half, especially when Abonyi's shot hit a post. But by then Overath had shot the Germans ahead from outside the box, Cullmann had added a second and Gerd Müller, with a near post header, the third. Australia finished without a goal in the finals, but they ended with a courageous point against Chile.

So to the crunch, the first ever meeting of East and West Germany in Hamburg. Rumours spread of terrorist rocket-launchers trained on the stadium, and police were everywhere. The East Germans packed their defence and kept only Sparwasser and Hoffman up in forward positions. Their strategy was the breakaway – and it paid off, but only after Grabowski had missed a great chance for West Germany and Müller had hit an East German post. Even so Kreische missed the easiest chance of all for East Germany before Sparwasser took a pass from the substitute Hamann, forced his way past Vogts and shot the winner past Maier.

Significantly, this took the East Germans through as winners of the group while the West Germans consequently avoided the Dutch until the Final. Skipper Franz Beckenbauer had since suggested this could have been decisive. Certainly, Holland were in impressive enough form in their qualifying group but they saved their real brilliance for the second round. Like West Germany, they enjoyed the cohesion of a nucleus of players from their club sides Ajax and Feyenoord. The attacking talent alongside Cruyff was fantastic—Johan Neeskens, Johnny Rep, Wim Van Hanegem and Rob Rensenbrink. They began brilliantly against Uruguay, winning with two Rep goals, stumbled against Sweden (drawing 0-0), then dispatched Bulgaria 4-1. The Swedes, who went through with them, could boast two tremendous strikers in Ralf Edstroem, now playing in Holland, the best header of a ball in the competition, and Roland Sandberg, his old Swedish clubmate. They shared their only three goals in the win over Bulgaria.

In Group 2, in Frankfurt, Brazil and Yugoslavia gave the 1974 finals the same start as those in Mexico and England before—a goalless draw. The caution of Brazil was astonishing; the skill and flexibility of the Yugoslavs should have won it for them by two or three goals. And if referee Rudi Scheurer of Switzerland had not ducked his responsibility, they would certainly have had a penalty when Acimovic was chopped down by two defenders. Brazil were going to earn a reputation for steel rather than skill, and they also survived a header from Yugoslavia's brilliant midfield general Branko Oblak which hit a post.

Scotland felt they had a real chance as they opened against the 'Leopards' of Zaire. But this was where they faltered. It was to be

opposite **Johan Cruyff, who came to West Germany with the title of the world's best player, in action in Holland's opening game against Uruguay.**

left above **Johan Neeskens scores from the penalty spot to open Holland's account in the 4-0 win over Bulgaria.**

left **Ralf Edstroem, Sweden's commanding centre forward, scores the last of Sweden's goals in the 3-0 defeat of Uruguay.**

above **Johnny Rep, who scored four goals for Holland during the finals.**

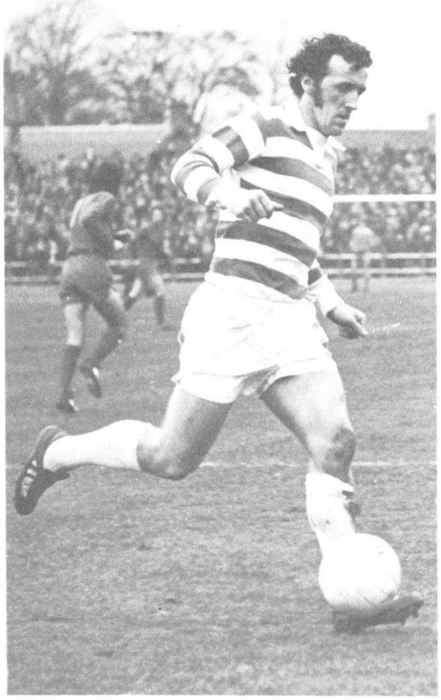

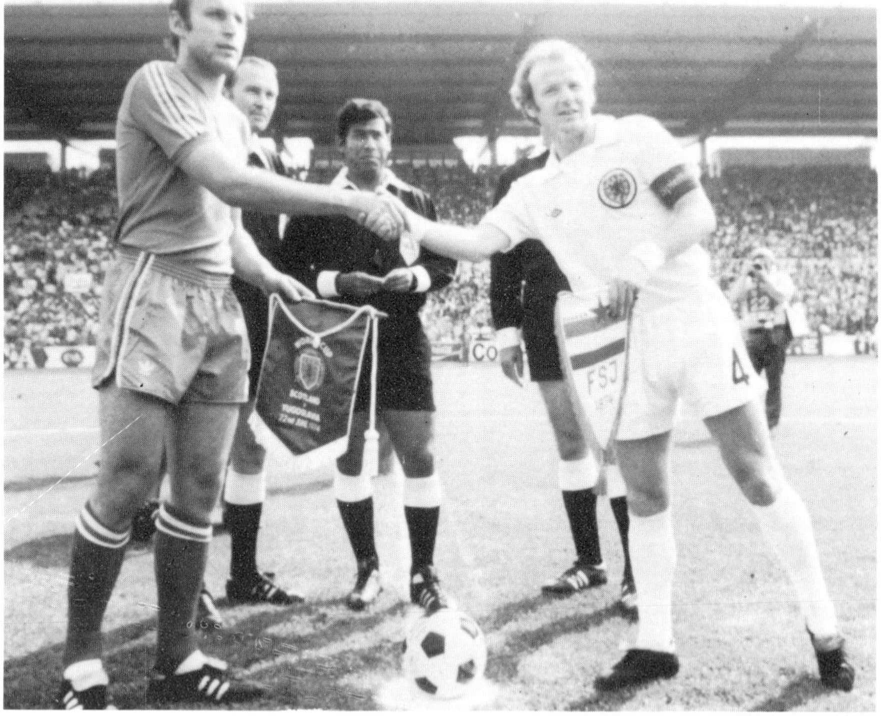
FSJ
4

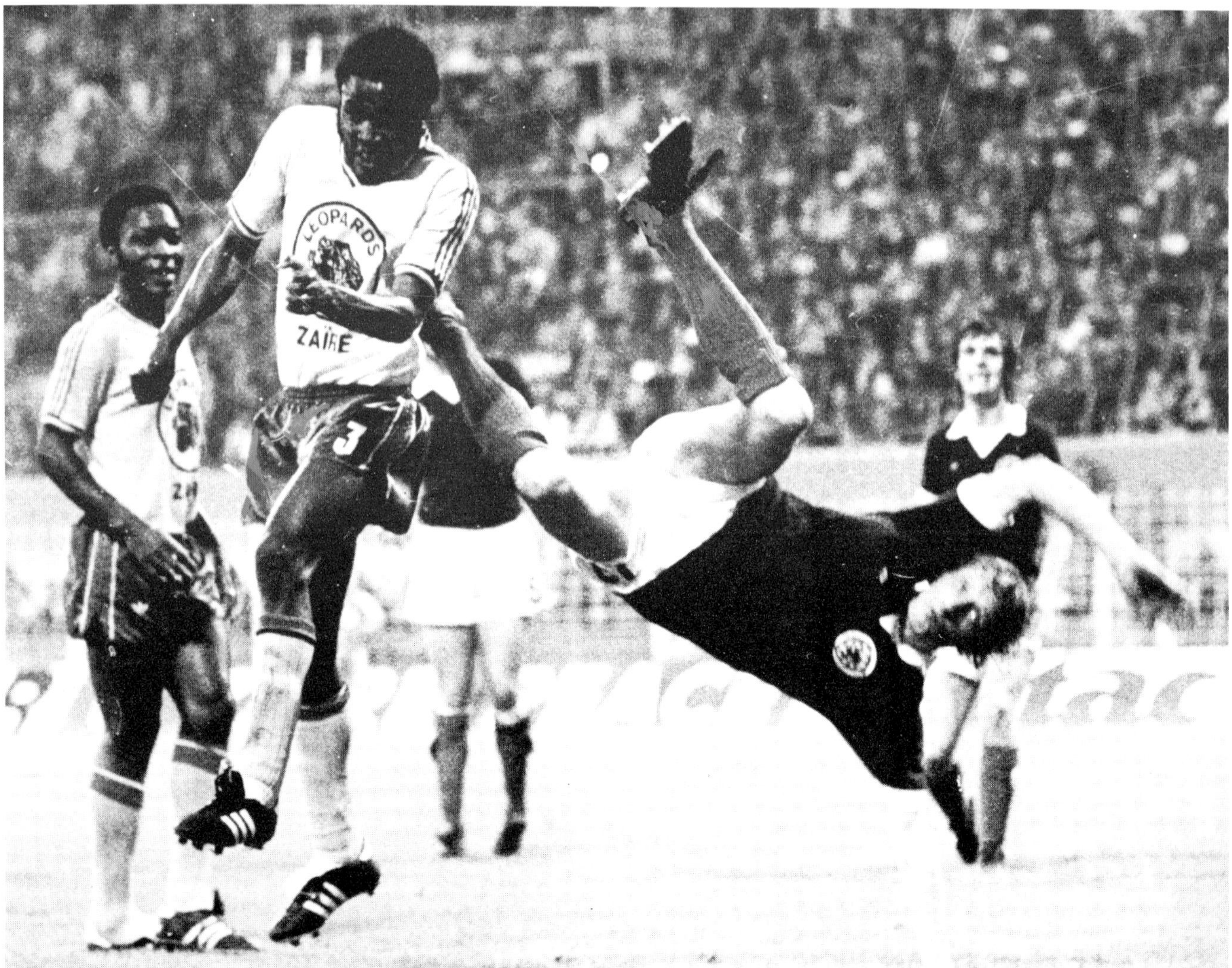
LEOPARDS
ZAÏRE
3

opposite, top left **One of unbeaten Scotland's best defenders in 1974, full back Danny McGrain.**

opposite, top right **Captains of Yugoslavia and Scotland, Dragan Dzajic and Billy Bremner, exchange pennants before the 1-1 draw.**

opposite below **Scottish veteran Denis Law in typical cartwheel action against Zaire.**

left **Billy Bremner was an inspiring Scottish captain, but Scotland were eliminated because they failed to score enough against Zaire in their opening match.**

below **Joe Jordan of Scotland was one of the most feared centre forwards of the 1974 tournament.**

a group where the three top teams drew against each other. So the decision rested on how easily they could all beat Zaire. Scotland managed 2-0, Brazil 3-0 and the Yugoslavs 9-0. It was no consolation to Scotland that they were the moral victors against both Brazil and Yugoslavia (although in this one they needed a late equaliser). They were eliminated on goal difference – the only unbeaten side in the whole tournament.

Group 4 looked explosive. It contained the Italians, strongly fancied and playing not far from home in Munich and Stuttgart; Argentina, with a track record of violence; the Poles, who had shown Wales that they could look after themselves well enough; and finally the unknowns from Haiti.

Italy began as if they could still not shed the shadow of 1966. Haiti's one known player, Emmanuel Sanon, breached their defence for the first time in thirteen internationals. Goalkeeper Dino Zoff had to pull the ball out of the net for the first time in 1,143 minutes of football. But Rivera, Benetti and Anastasi put the record straight with three later goals. For their part, Poland were the revelation of the group, winning all three games, despite the absence of their star striker Lubanski.

Their first match was against Argentina, who sparkled in their 3-2 defeat. Defensive errors proved far too costly for the Argentinians. Goalkeeper Carnevali gave Lato the first goal and Szarmach found acres of space to add a second from Lato's pass. Heredia came up to reduce the margin after half-time, but when Carnevali threw the ball straight out to Lato who gratefully added a third it was all over, despite Babington's final goal for Argentina.

Against Argentina, only a silly own goal by defender Perfumo, who diverted Benetti's cross from the left past Carnevali, earned Italy a 1-1 draw. Houseman, who got the goal, and Babington were outstanding. The Italians were now demoralised and they duly fell 2-1 to the Poles who had earlier put seven goals past Haiti. Kasperczak's crosses gave Szar-

above **Dzajic, Yugoslavia's brilliant left winger, in action against Brazil.**

left **Jerzy Gorgon, a giant in Poland's defence.**

opposite top **Emmanuel Sanon's goal for Haiti was the first against Italy in thirteen internationals, but he failed to prevent Pietro Anastasi scoring the third in Italy's 3-1 win.**

right **Poland's clever midfield general Kazimierz Deyna.**

far right **Penalty-saving expert, Poland's acrobatic goalkeeper Jan Tomaszewski.**

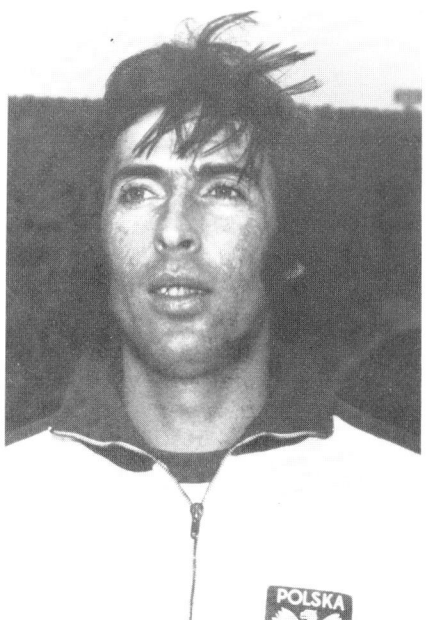

mach, with a header, and Deyna, with a volley, glorious goals for the winners. The Italians went home vowing they would change to a more positive style than 'catenaccio'–their traditional springboarding out of a basically defensive set-up. Argentina went through on goal difference with Poland. But there were stories afterwards that the Italians, who only needed a draw against Poland to survive, had offered the Poles bribes. Either way it had not worked.

As the tournament now divided into its two groups, Holland grew in stature and adventure with every game, winning all their games without conceding a goal. First victims were Argentina,

right **A goal for Poland's Szarmach. Italy's Francesco Morini fails to stop him heading in in Poland's 2-1 win.**

opposite right **The result of Szarmach's header. Dino Zoff dives but the ball is past him.**

below **Poland beat Haiti 7-0, and their hapless goalkeeper Henri Francillon can only look on in despair as Andrej Szarmach heads in the sixth.**

opposite below **Carlos Babington was one of Argentina's stars of 1974. Haitian goalkeeper Francillon and defender Vorbe fail to prevent this goal.**

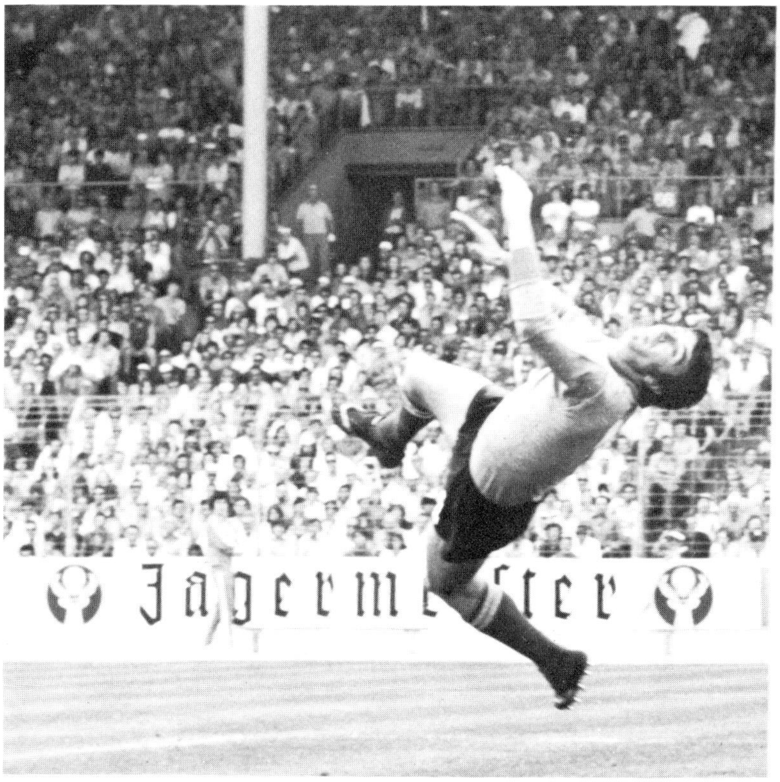

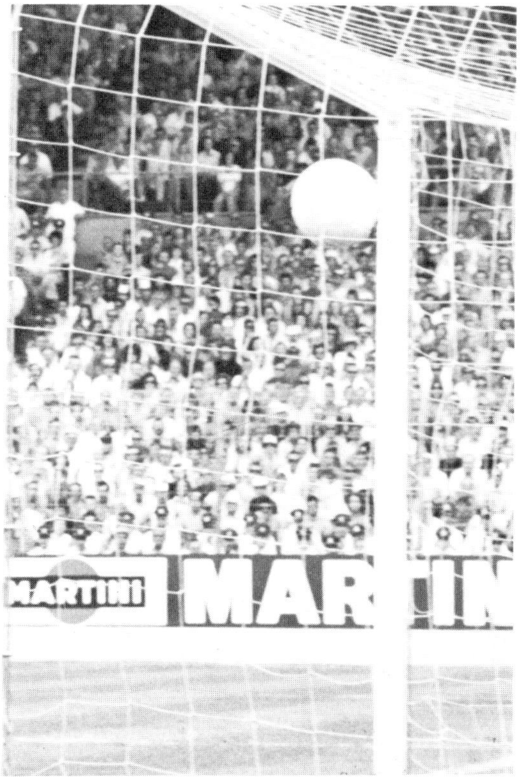
MARTINI

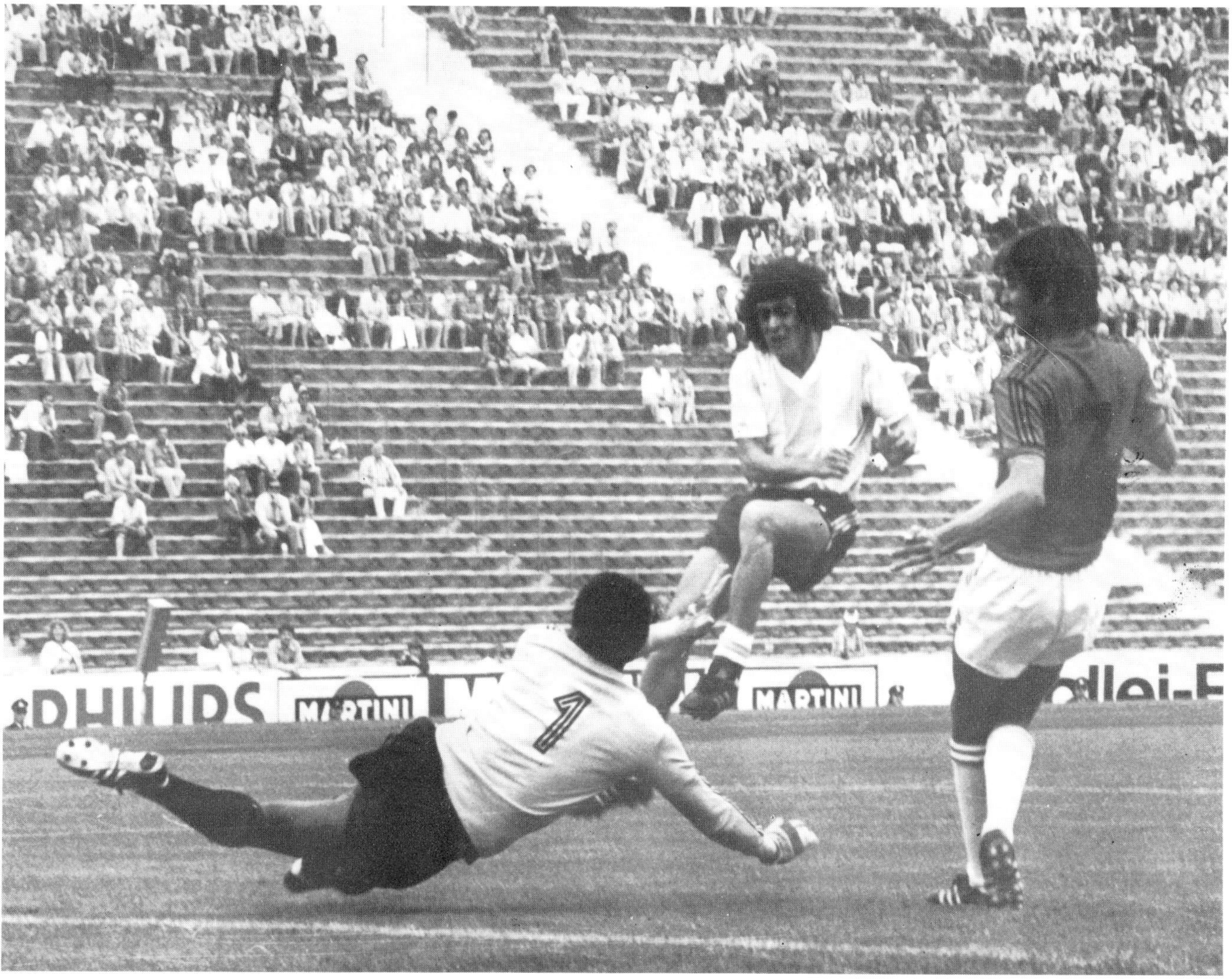
MARTINI
MARTINI

above **Holland beat East Germany, appearing for the first time in the finals, 2-0. Neeskens and Schnupphase in a duel for the ball.**

opposite above **Johan Neeskens scores the first goal for Holland in the match with Brazil. Luis Pereira's tackle is too late to intercept the shot from a narrow angle.**

opposite below **Holland's second goal. Johan Cruyff flies through the air to volley home a cross from the left.**

severely handicapped by the absence of Babington, suspended after three bookings. Holland ran riot and there were two goals for Cruyff in a 4-0 victory. The East Germans put Weise on Cruyff but it did not prevent Rensenbrink setting up the first goal for Neeskens and then scoring the second himself after a typical sweeping move. Holland now needed only a draw against Brazil to reach the final.

Brazil had beaten East Germany with a set-piece goal from Rivelino. And, although conceding their first goal of the tournament against Argentina, they won with another goal from Rivelino and one from Jairzinho – shades of 1970. It was sad though that they chose to combat the brilliant Dutch not with football but with violence. It was a shameful exhibition, and all the more shocking coming from Brazil. The brutal Luis Pereira was sent off as thrilling goals from Neeskens and Cruyff sent Holland through to the final.

West Germany and Poland were clearly going to dispute the other Final place. But Sweden's combination of veterans and amateurs gave them both a run for their money. It needed a penalty save by Tomaszewski and a goal from Lato, who went on to be top scorer in the finals, to see Poland through. West Germany had to come from behind to win *their* match with the Swedes 4-2, and might have struggled more if Larsson had not had to go off.

Both sides beat Yugoslavia as well, Poland rather luckily. Karasi need never have floored Szarmach for a penalty which Deyna converted. And then, after Karasi had made amends himself with an equaliser, the Slavs looked to be taking control when Lato's near-post header decided it. West Germany were far more impressive when they beat Yugoslavia 2-0. It could have been a much wider margin. As it was Breitner got the first and Müller the second. Beckenbauer was in imperious form.

So the final place would rest on the meeting of West Germany and Poland in Frankfurt on July 3, 1974. It was a day for watersport rather than football. The Frankfurt pitch was flooded and the kick-off had to be delayed over half an hour while the local fire service pumped off the bulk of the surface water. Conditions would not favour the Poles. They needed a win and the Germans, who needed only to draw, would surely have the edge in strength.

The Poles were the better team in the first half and Maier needed to be at his most acrobatic and daring to keep out a free kick by Gadocha and a breakaway shot by Lato. In the second-half, Holzenbein, the Frankfurt winger, was brought down in a sliding tackle by Zmuda – penalty. But, once

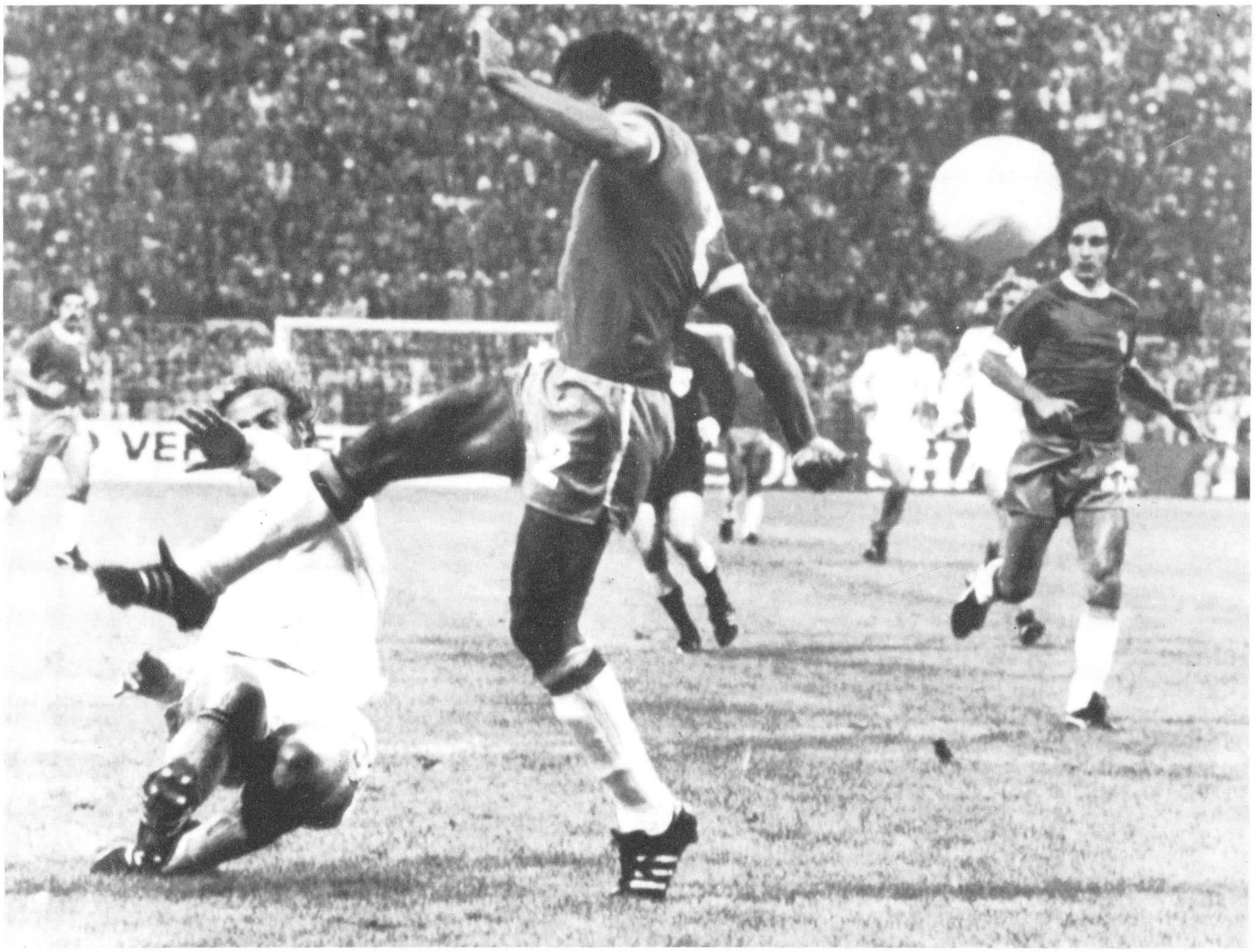

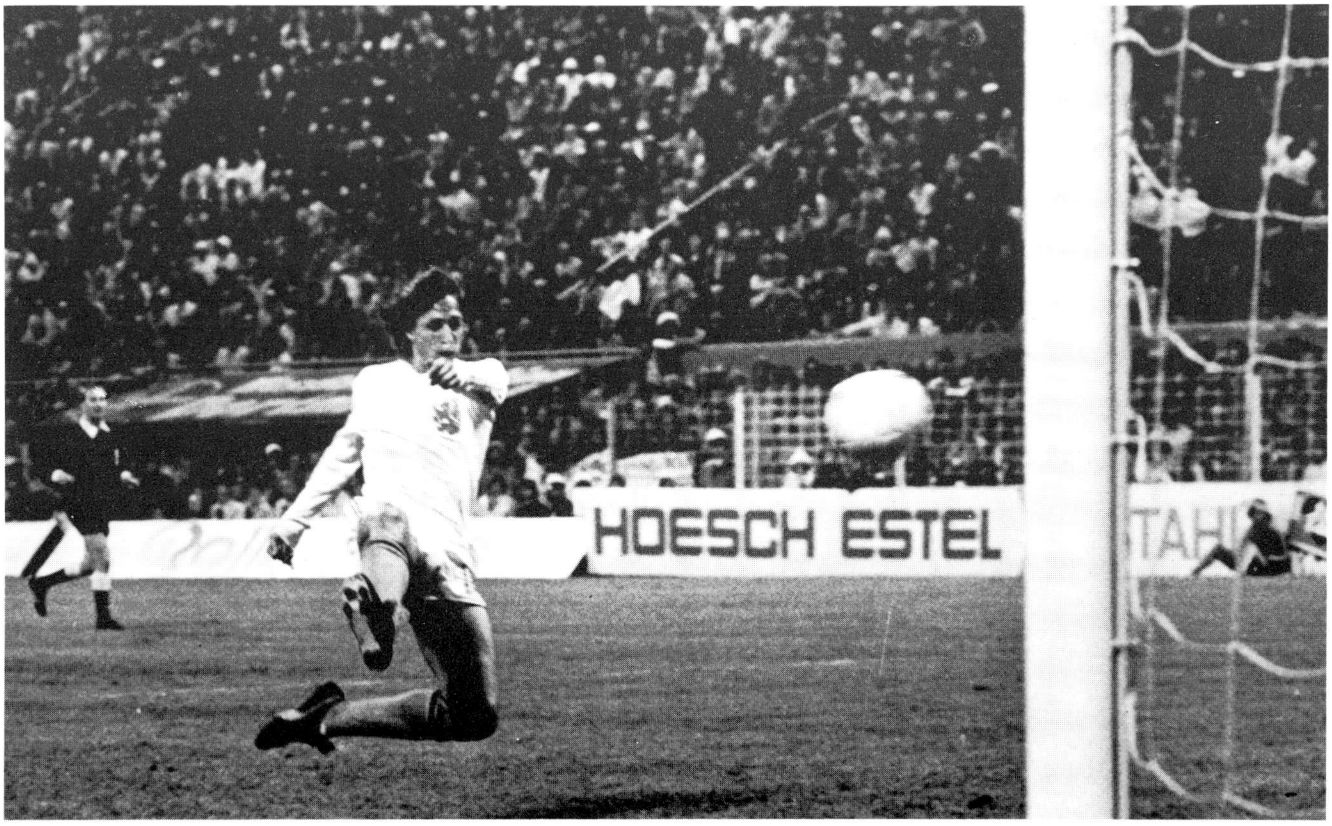
HOESCH ESTEL

left **West Germany fought an exciting match with Sweden. Wolfgang Overath scores West Germany's first through defenders Karlsson, Augustsson and Nordquist.**

left centre **Gerd Muller failed with this effort as Swedish goalkeeper Hellstroem smothered the ball.**

left bottom **The last of West Germany's four goals. Ule Hoeness slots a penalty past Hellstroem.**

right **Muller on the mark for West Germany against Yugoslavia. Maric's dive and Acimovic's tackle are both beaten.**

below **Grzegorz Lato of Poland beats Brazil's goalkeeper Leao to register a 1-0 win for Poland.**

below right **Polish players Zmuda and Gadocha shield the ball from Brazil's Jairzinho in the same match.**

87

top **Two of Holland's best players in the 1974 Final, Rudi Krol (left) and Van Hanegem (right).**

above **Central players in West Germany's team, Gerd Muller, the ace striker, and captain Franz Beckenbauer, the central defender and mid-field inspiration.**

again, the incredible Tomaszewski saved Poland from Hoeness's kick. Still, Holzenbein eventually provided the opening from which the inevitable Müller got the decisive goal. Poland went on to win third place by beating Brazil 1-0 in the play-off before the Final.

The stage was set. Now West Germany – like Uruguay in 1930, Italy in 1934, Brazil in 1950, Sweden in 1958 and England in 1966 – had merely to finish the job while the nation held its breath. And there could scarcely have been a more breathless start to the Final.

Holland kicked off and played a series of fifteen unbroken passes up to and across the face of the German penalty area. Suddenly the explosion came with Cruyff darting into the penalty area only to be brought crashing down by Hoeness. The English referee Jack Taylor pointed immediately to the spot. The crowd was stunned. Many could not bear to watch as Neeskens scored from the penalty. Ninety seconds gone, Holland one-up and surely on the way to a historic victory. But their poise did not hold.

After twenty-six minutes, Germany attacked down the left, Holzenbein cut into the penalty

left **The sensational start to the 1974 Final. Cruyff is brought down in the first minute as Berti Vogts moves in to tackle, and British referee Jack Taylor gives a penalty.**

above **Germany's equalizer in the 1974 Final also came from the penalty spot, scored by Paul Breitner.**

area and Jansen cut him down with the covering tackle. It was another penalty – and after Breitner scored from it, the Dutch were suddenly on the receiving end. Yet Cruyff set up a chance for Rep which could have restored Holland's lead and morale only for Rep to shoot straight at Maier. Six minutes later Germany scored what proved to be the winner.

Bonhof surged through on the right, beat Haan for pace and crossed to Müller who, at the second attempt, hooked his shot unerringly beyond the reach of Jongbloed. Holland dominated the second half. Breitner and Bonhof cleared off the German line and Maier in goal never faltered, even when Neeskens crashed a shot against his body. It was 'death or glory' stuff. And the final whistle gave all the glory to 'Kaiser' Franz Beckenbauer and his men, not forgetting the man who plotted and managed it all, Helmut Schoen. In direct descent from Sepp Herberger, he had built another triumph for Germany efficiency. Like Herberger's team in 1954, he had lost a battle, but won the war, and in the process had disposed of rivals with patently more skill but in the end less self-belief.

above **Gerd Muller** gets a flying header at the Dutch goal in the 1974 Final, but goalkeeper Jan Jongbloed made the save.

right **The winning goal in the Final.** Arie van Haan of Holland tries to tackle but Gerd Muller has already shot and the ball is on its way to the net.

opposite, above left **In Holland's great fight-back,** Cruyff heads the ball back into the centre where goalkeeper Maier and full back Vogts guard the goal.

opposite, above right **Sepp Maier** with the new World Cup, won by West Germany, after Brazil had kept the Jules Rimet trophy after their third win in 1970.

opposite below **Helmut Schoen,** the West German manager, with his winning squad and the World Cup.

## 10th WORLD CUP  West Germany, 1974

### GROUP 1

| | | | | |
|---|---|---|---|---|
| **West Germany** | (1)1 | Chile | (0)0 | |
| Breitner | | | | |
| **East Germany** | (0)2 | Australia | (0)0 | |
| Curran (og), Streich | | | | |
| **West Germany** | (2)3 | Australia | (0)0 | |
| Overath, Cullmann, Muller | | | | |
| **East Germany** | (0)1 | Chile | (0)1 | |
| Hoffmen | | Abumada | | |
| **Chile** | (0)0 | Australia | (0)0 | |
| **East Germany** | (0)1 | W. Germany | (0)0 | |
| Sparwasser | | | | |

| | P | W | D | L | F | A | Pts |
|---|---|---|---|---|---|---|---|
| East Germany | 3 | 2 | 1 | 0 | 4 | 1 | 5 |
| West Germany | 3 | 2 | 0 | 1 | 4 | 1 | 4 |
| Chile | 3 | 0 | 2 | 1 | 1 | 2 | 2 |
| Australia | 3 | 0 | 1 | 2 | 0 | 5 | 1 |

### GROUP 2

| | | | | |
|---|---|---|---|---|
| **Brazil** | (0)0 | Yugoslavia | (0)0 | |
| **Scotland** | (2)2 | Zaire | (0)0 | |
| Lorimer, Jordan | | | | |
| **Brazil** | (0)0 | Scotland | (0)0 | |
| **Yugoslavia** | (6)9 | Zaire | (0)0 | |
| Bajevic 3, Dzajic, Surjak, Katalinski, Bogicevic, Oblak, Petkovic | | | | |
| **Scotland** | (0)1 | Yugoslavia | (0)1 | |
| Jordan | | Karasi | | |
| **Brazil** | (1)3 | Zaire | (0)0 | |
| Jairzinho, Rivelino, Valdomiro | | | | |

| | P | W | D | L | F | A | Pts |
|---|---|---|---|---|---|---|---|
| Yugoslavia | 3 | 1 | 2 | 0 | 10 | 1 | 4 |
| Brazil | 3 | 1 | 2 | 0 | 3 | 0 | 4 |
| Scotland | 3 | 1 | 2 | 0 | 3 | 1 | 4 |
| Zaire | 3 | 0 | 0 | 3 | 0 | 14 | 0 |

### GROUP 3

| | | | | |
|---|---|---|---|---|
| **Netherlands** | (1)2 | Uruguay | (0)0 | |
| Rep 2 | | | | |
| **Sweden** | (0)0 | Bulgaria | (0)0 | |
| **Netherlands** | (0)0 | Sweden | (0)0 | |
| **Bulgaria** | (0)1 | Uruguay | (0)1 | |
| Bonev | | Pavoni | | |
| **Netherlands** | (2)4 | Bulgaria | (0)1 | |
| Neeskens (2 pens), Rep, De Jong | | Krol (og) | | |
| **Sweden** | (0)3 | Uruguay | (0)0 | |
| Edstroem 2, Sandberg | | | | |

| | P | W | D | L | F | A | Pts |
|---|---|---|---|---|---|---|---|
| Netherlands | 3 | 2 | 1 | 0 | 6 | 1 | 5 |
| Sweden | 3 | 1 | 2 | 0 | 3 | 0 | 4 |
| Bulgaria | 3 | 0 | 2 | 1 | 2 | 5 | 2 |
| Uruguay | 3 | 0 | 1 | 2 | 1 | 5 | 1 |

### GROUP 4

| | | | | |
|---|---|---|---|---|
| **Italy** | (0)3 | Haiti | (0)1 | |
| Rivera, Benetti, Anastasi | | Sanon | | |
| **Poland** | (2)3 | Argentina | (0)2 | |
| Lato 2, Szarmach | | Heredia, Babington | | |
| **Argentina** | (1)1 | Italy | (1)1 | |
| Houseman | | Perfumo (og) | | |
| **Poland** | (5)7 | Haiti | (0)0 | |
| Lato 2, Deyna, Szarmach 3, Gorgon | | | | |
| **Argentina** | (2)4 | Haiti | (0)1 | |
| Yazalde 2, Houseman, Ayala | | Sanon | | |
| **Poland** | (2)2 | Italy | (0)1 | |
| Szarmach, Deyna | | Capello | | |

| | P | W | D | L | F | A | Pts |
|---|---|---|---|---|---|---|---|
| Poland | 3 | 3 | 0 | 0 | 12 | 3 | 6 |
| Argentina | 3 | 1 | 1 | 1 | 7 | 5 | 3 |
| Italy | 3 | 1 | 1 | 1 | 5 | 4 | 3 |
| Haiti | 3 | 0 | 0 | 3 | 2 | 14 | 0 |

### GROUP A

| | | | | |
|---|---|---|---|---|
| **Brazil** | (0)1 | E. Germany | (0)0 | |
| Rivelino | | | | |
| **Netherlands** | (2)4 | Argentina | (0)0 | |
| Cruyff 2, Krol, Rep | | | | |
| **Netherlands** | (1)2 | E. Germany | (0)0 | |
| Neeskens, Rensenbrink | | | | |
| **Brazil** | (1)2 | Argentina | (1)1 | |
| Rivelino, Jairzinho | | Brindisi | | |
| **Netherlands** | (0)2 | Brazil | (0)0 | |
| Neeskens, Cruyff | | | | |
| **Argentina** | (1)1 | E. Germany | (1)1 | |
| Houseman | | Streich | | |

| | P | W | D | L | F | A | Pts |
|---|---|---|---|---|---|---|---|
| Netherlands | 3 | 3 | 0 | 0 | 8 | 0 | 6 |
| Brazil | 3 | 2 | 0 | 1 | 3 | 3 | 4 |
| East Germany | 3 | 0 | 1 | 2 | 1 | 4 | 1 |
| Argentina | 3 | 0 | 1 | 2 | 2 | 7 | 1 |

### GROUP B

| | | | | |
|---|---|---|---|---|
| **Poland** | (1)1 | Sweden | (0)0 | |
| Lato | | | | |
| **West Germany** | (1)2 | Yugoslavia | (0)0 | |
| Breitner, Muller | | | | |
| **Poland** | (1)2 | Yugoslavia | (1)1 | |
| Deyna (pen), Lato | | Karasi | | |
| **West Germany** | (0)4 | Sweden | (1)2 | |
| Overath, Bonhof, Grabowski, Hoeness (pen) | | Edstroem, Sandberg | | |
| **Sweden** | (1)2 | Yugoslavia | (1)1 | |
| Edstroem | | Surjek | | |
| **West Germany** | (0)1 | Poland | (0)0 | |
| Muller | | | | |

| | P | W | D | L | F | A | Pts |
|---|---|---|---|---|---|---|---|
| West Germany | 3 | 3 | 0 | 0 | 7 | 2 | 6 |
| Poland | 3 | 2 | 0 | 1 | 3 | 2 | 4 |
| Sweden | 3 | 1 | 0 | 2 | 4 | 6 | 2 |
| Yugoslavia | 3 | 0 | 0 | 3 | 2 | 6 | 0 |

**THIRD PLACE MATCH**: Munich 6.7.74
Attendance 70,000

| | | | | |
|---|---|---|---|---|
| **Poland** | (0)1 | Brazil | (0)0 | |
| Lato | | | | |

**FINAL**: Munich 7.7.74
Attendance 77,833

| | | | | |
|---|---|---|---|---|
| **W. Germany** | (2)2 | Netherlands | (1)1 | |
| Breitner (pen), Muller | | Neeskens (pen) | | |

**W. Germany**: Maier; Vogts, Schwarzenbeck, Beckenbauer, Breitner, Bonhof, Hoeness, Overath, Grabowski, Muller, Holzenbein
**Netherlands**: Jongbloed; Suurbier, Rijsbergen [De Jong], Haan, Krol, Jansen, Van Hanagem, Neeskens, Rep, Cruyff, Resenbrink [Van der Kerkhof]
**Referee**: Jack Taylor (England)

**LEADING SCORERS**
7—Lato (Poland)
5—Szarmach (Poland), Neeskens (Netherlands)
4—Rep (Netherlands), Edstroem (Sweden), Muller (West Germany)

91

# World Cup Top Twenty

| Country | Starts | 1(5pts) | 2(4) | 3(3) | 4(2) | Final Round(1) | Total |
|---|---|---|---|---|---|---|---|
| 1 Brazil | 10 | 3 | 1 | 1 | 1 | 4 | 28 |
| 2 W. Germany | 8 | 2 | 1 | 2 | 1 | 2 | 24 |
| 3 Italy | 8 | 2 | 1 | 0 | 0 | 5 | 19 |
| 4 Uruguay | 7 | 2 | 0 | 0 | 2 | 3 | 17 |
| 5 Hungary | 6 | 0 | 2 | 0 | 0 | 4 | 12 |
| 6 Czechoslovakia | 6 | 0 | 2 | 0 | 0 | 4 | 12 |
| 7 Sweden | 6 | 0 | 1 | 1 | 1 | 3 | 12 |
| 8 England | 6 | 1 | 0 | 0 | 0 | 5 | 10 |
| 9 Argentina | 6 | 0 | 1 | 0 | 0 | 5 | 9 |
| 10 Yugoslavia | 6 | 0 | 0 | 1 | 1 | 4 | 9 |
| 11 France | 6 | 0 | 0 | 1 | 0 | 5 | 8 |
| 12 Chile | 5 | 0 | 0 | 1 | 0 | 4 | 7 |
| 13 Mexico | 7 | 0 | 0 | 0 | 0 | 7 | 7 |
| 14 Holland | 3 | 0 | 1 | 0 | 0 | 2 | 6 |
| 15 Austria | 3 | 0 | 0 | 1 | 1 | 1 | 6 |
| 16 Switzerland | 6 | 0 | 0 | 0 | 0 | 6 | 6 |
| 17 USA | 3 | 0 | 0 | 1 | 0 | 2 | 5 |
| 18 Spain | 4 | 0 | 0 | 0 | 1 | 3 | 5 |
| 19 Russia | 4 | 0 | 0 | 0 | 1 | 3 | 5 |
| 20 Belgium | 5 | 0 | 0 | 0 | 0 | 5 | 5 |

NB: Highest placing in any tournament gives preference where points are level.

## Acknowledgements

The publishers thank the following who supplied the pictures for this book:
Allsport (Don Morley): 7, 40. Associated Press Ltd: front and back endpapers, 49 top, 52 bottom, 77 top left, 81 top, 82 top, 83, 85, 86 top and bottom, 87 bottom, 90 bottom. Owen Barnes: 50 top, 68 bottom, 69, 77 right, 78 top right, 80 bottom, 81 bottom, 88 top, 89 left, 91 top left. Central Press Ltd: 12, 27 right, 34 right, 38 bottom left, 41, 43, 46, 47, 48 bottom, 49 top left, 50 bottom, 52 top, 54, 55 top and bottom, 56 top, 57 top, 59 centre, 61, 62, 63 top, 67 top left, 75 bottom, 84, 86 centre, 87 top, 88 bottom, 91 bottom. Colorsport: 63 right, 75 top, 79, 80 top. Keystone Press Agency Ltd: 8, 10, 11, 13, 14, 15, 16, 18, 19, 20, 21, 22, 23, 24, 25, 26, 27 left, 28, 29, 30, 31, 32, 34 left, 35, 36 top and bottom right, 37, 38 top and bottom right, 39, 42, 44 top, 44-45, 48 top and centre, 55 centre, 57 bottom, 59 top, 60 top, 60 bottom right, 64 bottom, 65, 67 top right, 68 top, 70, 73, 74, 76, 77 bottom left, 82 bottom, 88-89, 90 top, 91 top right, 93 left. Popperfoto: title-page, 36 bottom left. Press Association: 49 bottom, 56 bottom, 93 right. Pressens Bild (Stockholm): 38-39 top. Sportapics Ltd: 78 top left. Sporting Pictures (UK) Ltd: 64 top right. Syndication International: 51, 53, 58, 59 bottom, 60 bottom left, 63 bottom left, 64 top left, 66, 67 bottom, 71, 72, 78 bottom.

The current World Cup first fought for in 1974 and won by West Germany, is twenty inches high, cast in gold, and weighs eleven pounds.

The first World Cup, the Jules Rimet trophy, is now held in perpetuity by Brazil, who won it for the third time in 1970. It is twelve inches high and solid gold.